FRIENDS

FRIENDS

by
KOBO ABE

Translated from
the Japanese
by Donald Keene

GROVE PRESS, INC., NEW YORK

This translation is dedicated to I.L.

This play was first performed in the Kinokuniya Hall, Tokyo, on March 15, 1967. The performance was directed by Masahiko Naruse.

MIDDLE DAUGHTER, *twenty-four years old; a trim-looking, sweet girl who gives the impression of being a crystallization of good will*

GRANDMOTHER, *eighty years old*

FATHER, *a gentleman who at first glance might be taken for a clergyman; he wears a worn but quite respectable suit and carries a briefcase*

MOTHER, *her old-fashioned hat and glasses become her*

YOUNGER SON, *he once won a prize as an amateur boxer; he carries a guitar under one arm and a suitcase in the other*

ELDER SON, *clever, but frail-looking and rather gloomy; formerly a private detective; he carries suitcases in both hands when he enters*

ELDEST DAUGHTER, *thirty years old; a prospective old maid who still preserves her dreams of being raped by some man*

MAN, *thirty-one years old; section head in a commercial firm*

YOUNGEST DAUGHTER, *a little devil, though she doesn't look it*

MIDDLE-AGED POLICEMAN

YOUNG POLICEMAN

BUILDING SUPERINTENDENT, *a woman*

FIANCÉE, *she works in the same office as* MAN; *looks like a city girl*

REPORTER, *formerly a reporter for a weekly magazine*

FRIENDS

The curtain rises to the sweetly seductive melody of "The Broken Necklace." (Music by Takeshi Inomata.)

> *Night time in the big city—*
> *Now that the string is broken, the beads of the*
>   *necklace*
> *Scatter here and scatter there*
> *In every direction.*
> *Poor broken necklace, where is the breast that*
>   *warmed you once?*
> *When did you leave it, where has it gone?*
> *Little lost beads, little lost beads.*

Two large, partition-like walls meet in a "V" at the middle of the stage. Shadows of human figures, four each from left and right, appear on the walls and, to the rhythm of the music, gradually grow larger, until in the end they seem to loom like giants over the audience.

As the music comes to an end, the owners of the shadows reveal themselves from the wings on both sides. The composition of this family of eight could hardly be more average, but one senses something peculiar about its members. They move mechanically, nobody as yet showing any expression on his face.

MIDDLE DAUGHTER *steps forth from the group and advances to the center of the stage. The music should continue, but without words.*

MIDDLE DAUGHTER (*taking up the words of the song that has
been heard, her voice pleading and romantic*): But we can't
just leave them to their fate. We'll gather up those poor
little beads. Yes, we'll gather them up and run a new string
through them. (*She turns to* GRANDMOTHER.) We can do it,
Grandma, can't we?

GRANDMOTHER (*in a completely matter-of-fact tone*): Of course
we can. That's our job, isn't it?

MIDDLE DAUGHTER (*turning back to audience and continuing her
previous remarks*): It's wrong for there to be lost children
and lonely people. It's all wrong. But you can't make a
necklace without running a string through the beads. (*She
turns to* FATHER.) We'll be the string for the necklace.
Won't we, Father?

FATHER (*with a look of having heard this before*): Don't you
think I know it already, that being a string is our job?

MIDDLE DAUGHTER (*singing to the music*):
　　Where is the breast that warmed you once?
　　When did you leave it, where has it gone?
　　Little lost beads, little lost beads.

YOUNGEST DAUGHTER *suddenly gives a loud sneeze that
stops the music.*

MOTHER: My poor darling. (*To the others, reproachfully.*) If
we don't settle down somewhere soon, it'll be ten o'clock
before we know it.

YOUNGER SON: That's right. (*He yawns ostentatiously.*) I for
one have had enough of this gabbing.

ELDER SON (*sharply*): Don't talk like a fool. It's our job, isn't it?

ELDEST DAUGHTER (*without expression*): That's right. It's our
job.

The music begins again.

MIDDLE DAUGHTER (*resuming her exalted tone*): And that's
why we must go on. We must search out all the lonely

people and offer them our love and friendship. We are the messengers of love who can heal their loneliness. We must sniff out the faint wisps of sadness that escape like drops of starlight from the windows of the city, and go there with our gift of joy. (*She spreads her arms open as if introducing the family to the audience.*) Yes, we are the angels of broken necklaces.

Each member of the family simultaneously shines a flashlight from below on his face and smiles timidly. The contrast with the mood of what has preceded should be as strong as possible.

Blackout.

. . . SCENE TWO

The partitions are drawn aside to reveal Man's room. The furniture and household accessories should all be of one color, either a reddish brown or gray.

A door leads to the kitchen at stage-right front. At stage-left rear a door leads to another room. The entrance door to the apartment is at stage-left front. Next to the door, in the hall, is a rather elaborate coat rack. (This rack will later be used as a cage; it must therefore have suitable vertical and horizontal supports.) All the furnishings, including the doors, should be simplified and abbreviated as much as possible.

MAN *sits at the desk. He wears a jacket and jiggles his leg as he telephones. The telephone is the only real object in the room.*

MAN: Well, that's about all for now. I'll call you later on to say good night . . . What? It has yellow spots? Sounds like an alley cat, doesn't it? . . . No, I'm sorry. I assure you, I have absolute confidence in your taste . . . Oh, just a second. (*He removes the receiver from his ear and listens.*) No, it wasn't anything. I can't imagine anyone would come visiting me now, at this hour of the night . . . Yes, isn't that what I've been saying all along? Next payday I'd like you to move in here for good. You should have your things packed and ready by then.

The eight members of the family approach slowly and hesitantly, walking on tiptoe.

It sounds like rain? Yes, maybe it is raining. It couldn't be footsteps—it'd take too many people for that. You know, the insurance agent in the apartment below mine is a nut for poker . . . Of course the noise has nothing to do with me.

The footsteps suddenly grow louder. MAN *cocks his head and listens. The family enters from stage right and crosses stage front in a single line.* YOUNGER SON, *who has in the meantime passed his guitar to* ELDER SON, *goes past the entrance to Man's apartment, then turns back; at which all the others stop in their tracks.* FATHER *and* YOUNGER SON *stand on either side of the entrance.* FATHER *takes out a notebook and, after thumbing through the pages, compares what he finds with the name on the door. He nods and gives the signal to* MIDDLE DAUGHTER, *who is standing behind him. She comes forward and stands at the door, then knocks gently.*

MAN: Say, it's at my place! (*He glances hurriedly at his watch.*) Must be a telegram, at this hour of the night. (MIDDLE DAUGHTER *knocks again and he calls to other side of the door.*) ·I'll be with you in a minute! (*The family is visibly relieved. He speaks into the telephone.*) I'll go out and have a look. I'll call you later. Here's a kiss. (*He makes a noise with his lips and puts down the telephone.*)

. . . SCENE THREE

GRANDMOTHER, *having slipped around from behind* MIDDLE DAUGHTER, *peeps through the keyhole. She sees* MAN *coming to the door.*

GRANDMOTHER: My goodness—what a handsome man!
FATHER: Shhh! (*He takes* GRANDMOTHER *by her sleeve and pulls her back.*)
MAN: Who is it? Who's there?
MIDDLE DAUGHTER (*in a girlish voice*): Excuse me, please. I'm sorry to bother you so late.
MAN: Who is it, please? (*He is disarmed to discover the visitor is a young woman, but is all the more suspicious.*)
MIDDLE DAUGHTER: I'm so sorry. I intended to come earlier.

MAN *shakes his head doubtfully, but eventually yields to curiosity and opens the door a little. Instantly* YOUNGER SON *inserts his foot into the opening.* FATHER *takes the door knob and pulls the door open. The family, moving into action, assembles before the door.* MAN, *dumfounded, stands rooted.*

MIDDLE DAUGHTER: Oh, that's a relief! You hadn't gone to bed yet, had you?
FATHER (*in the tone of an old friend*): Of course not! The young folks these days are night owls, all of them.
MOTHER (*pushing* GRANDMOTHER *from behind*): Shall we go inside, Grandma? The night air is bad for you.
MAN (*his voice choked*): Who are you, anyway?
GRANDMOTHER (*ignoring* MAN *and starting to go in*): Oh, dear, it's pretty bare, isn't it?

ELDEST DAUGHTER (*exhibiting strong curiosity*): What do you
    expect? It's a bachelor apartment, after all.
MIDDLE DAUGHTER: That's right. And that's why it's so im-
    portant somebody come and help him.
MAN (*baffled*): Just a minute, please. I wonder if you haven't
    got the wrong party.
ELDER SON (*with a melancholy smile*): I used to work for a
    detective agency, you know.
MAN: But still—
YOUNGEST DAUGHTER: I'm cold.
MOTHER: Poor darling. You'll take an aspirin and get to bed
    early.

> MOTHER, *her arms around* YOUNGEST DAUGHTER, *propels*
> GRANDMOTHER *into the apartment.* MAN *tries to prevent*
> *her, but* YOUNGER SON *sees an opening and darts inside.*

MAN: What do you mean, breaking in, without even taking off
    your shoes?
YOUNGER SON: Oh—sorry. (*He removes his shoes.*)

> *The family takes advantage of Man's distraction to surge*
> *into the apartment in one wave.* FATHER, *the last in, shuts*
> *the door behind him and turns the key.* MAN, *in face of*
> *the concerted action of the eight of them, is powerless to*
> *resist. The members of the family scatter around the room*
> *with a kind of professional competence, neatly surrounding*
> MAN. *They flash at him their usual bashful smiles. They*
> *seem to have got the better of him.*

MAN: What's the big idea? It's enough to give a man the creeps.
FATHER (*unruffled*): Please, I beg you, don't get so upset.
MAN: If you've got some business with me, how about explain-
    ing exactly what it is?
FATHER: It puts us in an awkward position if you're going to
    turn on us that way . . . (*He looks around from one to*
    another of the family as if enlisting their support.)

MAN (*excitedly*): Puts you in an awkward position! You break in, without warning, on a total stranger, and you say it puts you in an awkward position! I'm the one who has something to complain about.

ELDER SON (*taps on the wall*): Pretty good! The walls have been soundproofed.

ELDEST DAUGHTER: It's freezing in here. Doesn't he have an electric heater, I wonder.

MAN (*unable to take any more*): Stop loitering around my apartment! All of you, get out of here! Now!

YOUNGER SON (*coolly*): Why, I feel as if we weren't wanted.

MAN: That's not surprising, is it? Of all the crassness!

YOUNGEST DAUGHTER *peeps into the back room.*

YOUNGEST DAUGHTER: Look, there's another room here.

GRANDMOTHER: It won't be easy dividing the space with only two rooms for nine people. (*She goes up beside* YOUNGEST DAUGHTER *and examines the other room with her.*)

MIDDLE DAUGHTER: We can't be fussy, you know. We didn't come here for our amusement.

MAN *stands at the door to the back room, blocking it. He is bewildered and uneasy.*

MAN: Out with all of you, and right now! If you refuse to go, I'll charge you with trespassing.

YOUNGEST DAUGHTER (*with an exaggerated show of terror*): Oh, he scares me!

MOTHER (*admonishingly*): There's nothing for you to be afraid of. He's really a very nice man. There, just look at his face. He's just pretending to frighten you, that's all.

GRANDMOTHER: That's right. He's what I'd call a handsome man. If I were only ten years younger . . .

MAN: I've had all I can stand! (*He starts to lift the telephone.*)

FATHER (*quietly restraining him*): Now calm yourself. You

seem to be under some terrible misapprehension. You're making such a fuss anybody might think we intended to do you some harm.

MAN: What do you intend, if not to harm me?

FATHER: Why should you say such a thing?

MAN: You're in a stranger's house here.

FATHER (*with an expression of dismay*): A stranger's house?

ELDER SON (*contemptuously*): A stranger's house! He certainly takes a very narrow view of things.

MAN: But, as a matter of fact, we are strangers, aren't we?

FATHER (*soothing him*): You mustn't get so worked up over each little thing. Have you never heard the saying that being brothers marks the first step on the way to being strangers? That means, if you trace strangers back far enough you'll find they were once brothers. What difference does it make if we're strangers? A little thing like that shouldn't upset you.

MOTHER: Yes, when you get to know us better you'll see we're just so relaxed and easy-going it's positively funny. (*She laughs.*)

MAN: Don't act silly. Whatever you may think, the fact is, this is my apartment.

ELDEST DAUGHTER: That's obvious, isn't it? If it weren't your apartment, you wouldn't be here.

YOUNGER SON: And if it weren't your apartment do you suppose we'd have listened in silence all this time to your belly-aching?

MIDDLE DAUGHTER: I thought I told you to lay off him.

YOUNGER SON: I apologize. The fact is, I have a wee bit of a hangover. Damn it!

YOUNGER SON *shadowboxes briefly to cover his confusion.* MIDDLE DAUGHTER, *acting as if she has suddenly noticed it, puts out her hand to remove a bit of wool fluff from Man's jacket.* ELDEST DAUGHTER *tries to beat her to it. But*

MAN *shrinks back from both of them, and neither is successful.* YOUNGEST DAUGHTER *chooses this moment to disappear into the kitchen.*

ELDEST DAUGHTER: I'm going to take off my coat, if you don't mind.

FATHER: Yes, we can't go on standing around this way indefinitely. Why don't we sit down and discuss things in a more relaxed mood?

They all remove their coats and hats. YOUNGER SON *also removes his jacket. Eldest Daughter's dress rather emphasizes her physique.*

MAN *steps forward resolutely, pushes* FATHER *aside, and picks up the telephone and dials with an air of determination.*

MAN: One, one, zero. (*He pauses, his finger inserted in the zero.*) Leave at once! Otherwise, I have only to release my finger and I'll be connected.

YOUNGER SON: To the police?

ELDEST DAUGHTER: Aren't you carrying things a bit too far?

FATHER (*perplexed*): It's a misunderstanding . . . a complete misunderstanding.

MAN: I have no time to bandy words with you. I'll give you until I count ten, that's all. I advise you to start getting ready. (*He starts to count slowly.*)

YOUNGER SON *stands menacingly before* MAN. *He looks at the family to see whether they want him to go ahead.*

FATHER (*sharply*): Stop! I forbid you to use violence.

MOTHER: Yes, we don't want people saying bad things about us. Stop it!

ELDER SON: How about, as a last resort, abiding by the will of the majority?

Man's attention is caught by the words "will of the major-ity." He slows down the speed of his counting.

ELDEST DAUGHTER: Even if we win a majority decision, it'd still be picking on someone weaker than us, wouldn't it?

ELDER SON: Don't be an idiot. The will of the majority means . . .

FATHER: Let's drop the whole matter. We know which side is going to win anyway. There aren't any thrills in this game.

GRANDMOTHER: Where might is master, justice is servant.

MIDDLE DAUGHTER (*somewhat uneasy*): What do you intend to do, anyway?

MAN: That's what I'd like to know. When I count one more, that'll make ten.

FATHER: It can't be helped. If you think it's absolutely necessary, do whatever you think best. It won't be very pleasant, but who knows?—it may prove more effective in bringing you to your senses than repeating the same old arguments.

MAN: Don't try to intimidate me! You're prepared, I take it? I'm really phoning the police.

FATHER: Go right ahead.

MAN (*releasing his finger from the dial emphatically*): Don't say I didn't warn you!

MOTHER (*sighs*): It's true, just as they say, a child never knows its parent's love.

MIDDLE DAUGHTER (*sighs*): This is the test run.

. . . SCENE FOUR

The telephone rings at the other end, then stops as the call is put through. The members of the family betray their tension in their expressions as they stand around the telephone. YOUNGER SON *puts a cigarette in his mouth.* GRANDMOTHER, *with an*

obsequious smile, tries to snatch away the cigarette, but
YOUNGER SON *brusquely pushes her hand aside and lights the*
cigarette. MAN *is worked up, but he keeps himself on guard*
against the family.

MAN : I'm sorry to bother you, but I've been intruded on by a
crazy outfit . . . No, it's not exactly a burglary . . . But
there are eight of them. I've tried in every way I know to
persuade them to leave, but they absolutely refuse to listen
. . . No, it's not a vendetta or anything like that. They're
total strangers . . . Yes, forced entry would be about right.
I suppose you could call it a kind of burglary in that sense
. . . That's right, eight of them . . . I? I'm all alone . . .
Will you? Sorry to bother you. The place—it's a little hard
to explain. Would you mind telephoning 467-0436 and
asking the superintendent for directions. That's her number. My name is Homma and I'm in Apartment 12 . . .
No, I don't think there's any immediate danger of violence,
but there's no telling under the circumstances . . . Yes,
I'd appreciate that. I'll be waiting for you . . . (*He
heaves a sigh and puts down the telephone.*)

ELDER SON, YOUNGER SON, *and* ELDEST DAUGHTER *smile to
themselves, each with obvious satisfaction.*

FATHER (*admonishingly*) : There's nothing to smile about!
I'm sure he was quite in earnest in doing what he did.
ELDER SON : But how can I help smiling? Burglary, he called
it! Burglary! If a cat denounced a mouse as a burglar you
couldn't keep the mouse from smiling just by telling him
he shouldn't.
ELDEST DAUGHTER : I realize of course he doesn't mean any
harm.
YOUNGER SON (*imitating Man's voice*) : Yes, sir. There are
eight of them, but I am all alone.

Kobo Abe

The members of the family start giggling again.

MAN (*challenging them*): Don't be so stubborn. You still have a few minutes left before the patrol car comes. I advise you not to waste your last chance.

YOUNGEST DAUGHTER *sticks her head out from the kitchen. Her face is smeared around the mouth with something she has been eating.* GRANDMOTHER *quickly surmises what has happened.*

GRANDMOTHER: Look at that! She's been nibbling something in the kitchen.

YOUNGEST DAUGHTER (*wiping her mouth and singing out*): The menu for tonight is two bottles of milk, six eggs, a loaf of bread, one bag of popcorn, one slice of mackerel, a pickle and some relish, two slices of frozen whalemeat, salad oil, and the usual spices.

YOUNGER SON: Quite a sweet tooth, hasn't he? Is there nothing in the way of liquor?

YOUNGEST DAUGHTER: Now that you mention it, there were two bottles of beer. That's all, I think.

YOUNGER SON: That's fine. I wanted a hair of the dog that bit me. (*He claps his hands in anticipation.*)

MOTHER: You can't drink it alone. We've got to save it to drink a toast to our new friendship.

ELDER SON: It's certainly not much of a menu in any case. You could find a better selection at a roadside diner.

MIDDLE DAUGHTER: Leave worrying about dinner to me. Those ingredients are more than enough for me to make quite a decent soup. (*She goes to the kitchen.*)

MAN: At last you've shown yourselves in your true colors. Out and out robbery is what I'd call it. The police will be here any minute. How do you plan to explain yourselves?

FATHER (*calmly*): You'll find out soon enough, when the time comes.

MAN: What will I find out?

ELDEST DAUGHTER: There's nothing for us to explain, is there? We're not doing anything we feel especially ashamed of.

MAN: Well, can you beat that? You talk as if you have the right to install yourselves in here. On what grounds can you justify—

MOTHER *pauses in her unpacking of her suitcase.*

MOTHER: But you're all alone here, aren't you?

MIDDLE DAUGHTER (*through the kitchen door*): It's terrible being alone. It's the worst thing that can happen to anybody.

ELDEST DAUGHTER: Yes, loneliness is bad for a person. In the first place, it makes you lose all resilience.

MAN: Supposing that's true, what business is it of yours?

FATHER: We're your friends. We can't abandon you, can we?

MAN: My friends?

FATHER: Of course we are. There are millions, even tens of millions of people in this city. And all of them are total strangers . . . Everywhere you look you see nothing but strangers . . . Don't you think that's frightening? There's no getting around it, we all need friends. Friends to help us, friends to encourage us.

GRANDMOTHER: In traveling, a companion; in life, sympathy. A wonderful thing, isn't it?

YOUNGER SON (*to* FATHER): Can't I have just one bottle of beer?

MAN (*nearly screaming*): I've had enough! I'm quite happy being alone. I'll thank you to stop your uncalled-for meddling. I don't want your sympathy. I'm enjoying my life just the way it is.

FATHER (*hesitantly*): But in general it's true, isn't it, that lunatics claim that they alone are sane?

MAN: Lunatics?

FATHER: Forgive me. I was using the word entirely by way of a simile.

MAN: As long as you're on the subject of lunatics, the description suits you all very well.

FATHER: Of course, it's difficult to define what we mean by a lunatic.

MOTHER *sits before the mirror and begins to apply vanishing cream.*

MOTHER: Nobody actually knows himself as well as he *thinks* he does.

ELDEST DAUGHTER (*suddenly clapping her hands*): That's right! I just remembered, I know a shop where they sell neckties that would look marvelous on you. I'll take you there the next time I go.

MOTHER (*reproving*): Instead of talking about such things you'd do better if you started helping in the kitchen. My stomach is beginning to tell me I need something to eat.

ELDEST DAUGHTER (*sulking*): Lend me your nail polish remover, will you?

GRANDMOTHER: I'm in charge of dividing up the jam!

MAN: Who the hell *are* you all anyway?

YOUNGER SON (*with an air of arrogant assurance*): I'll tell you this once and for all—the most important thing for anybody to learn is how to get along with other people. A man who can get along with other people will stay out of trouble.

ELDER SON: It has been proven statistically that most criminals are anti-social.

FATHER: Be that as it may, please trust in us, and feel secure in your trust as a passenger on a great ocean liner. I'm certain that one day you'll need us and be grateful to us.

MAN: I've had all I can stand of your high-pressure salesmanship. Of all the colossal nerve!

FATHER: But we have no choice. You consider yourself to be a human being, don't you? It stands to reason, then, that it is your privilege, and also your duty to live in a manner worthy of a human being.

YOUNGER SON *begins to strum the melody of "The Broken Necklace" on his guitar.* MIDDLE DAUGHTER *emerges from the kitchen and begins to sing the song, still peeling a carrot. The peel hangs down to the floor in a long, unbroken coil.*

MIDDLE DAUGHTER:

> Night time in the big city—
> Now that the string is broken, the beads of the necklace
> Scatter here and scatter there
> In every direction.
> Poor broken necklace, where is the breast that warmed
> you once?
> When did you leave it, where has it gone?
> Little lost beads, little lost beads.

. . . SCENE FIVE

Two policemen are led to the door of the apartment by the SUPERINTENDENT *who is a woman. The policemen have apparently been dropped some sort of hint by the* SUPERINTENDENT; *at any rate, they seem uncommonly lax in their demeanor.*

It may be that the SUPERINTENDENT *has been on bad terms with the* MAN, *or that she may already have been bought over by the family; or it simply may be that she is pretending to be neutral for fear of getting involved—this is not clear.*

The SUPERINTENDENT *points out the door of the Man's apartment and starts to make a hurried exit, but the* MIDDLE-AGED POLICEMAN, *with a wry smile, plucks her back by the sleeve, his gesture suggesting a man catching a bug. The* YOUNG

POLICEMAN *puts his ear to the door and listens to the sounds emanating from within, consulting his wristwatch as he does so. Then, with great deliberation, he presses the bell next to the door.*

MAN *rushes to the door in response to the bell, all but knocking down the members of the family nearest to him (probably* GRANDMOTHER *and* MIDDLE DAUGHTER), *and pushes the door open. This action barely misses causing the* YOUNG POLICEMAN *to fall on his ear.*

MAN (*flurried, but with great eagerness*) : Oh, I'm sorry. Well, this will give you an idea of the situation. Come in, please, and have a look for yourself. The culprits are still holding out. I'm glad you got here in time. Oh, there are two of you? (*He notices* SUPERINTENDENT.) It's good to have you along too, to back me up. Please step right in. Don't mind about me.

The policemen and SUPERINTENDENT, *at his urging, go inside. The* MIDDLE-AGED POLICEMAN, *standing at center, runs his eyes professionally over the family. They betray no noticeable agitation. With absolute self-possession, they all stop whatever they were doing and return the policeman's suspicious stare with smiles and nods that all but overflow with a sincerity that could only come from the heart.*

MAN (*excitedly*) : They're eight of them altogether. The other one's in the kitchen.

YOUNGEST DAUGHTER *enters from the kitchen, wiping her mouth. She obviously has been nibbling again.* GRANDMOTHER *gives the girl a severe look and starts to scold, but* FATHER *and* ELDER SON *restrain her casually.*

YOUNGEST DAUGHTER : Here I am.

MOTHER: Say hello to the gentlemen.

YOUNGEST DAUGHTER (*in a childish, bashful manner*): Good evening.

MIDDLE-AGED POLICEMAN (*confused*): Hmmm. Well then, what's the offense?

MAN (*failing to catch the words*): Excuse me?

YOUNG POLICEMAN: Their offense—what specific injury have you suffered?

MAN (*indignant*): I don't have to specify, do I? You've caught them red-handed in the act.

The members of the family continue to smile, quite unperturbed. Their smiles are confident and beyond all suspicion. MAN, *however, has become so upset by the passive attitude of the policemen that he is flustered and does not seem to have become aware of the performance the family is putting on.* MIDDLE-AGED POLICEMAN *looks as if the smile tactics of the family have got the better of him. He lowers his eyes to his notebook and reads as he speaks.*

MIDDLE-AGED POLICEMAN: According to the complaint, illegal entry has occurred on these premises.

MAN: That's it precisely!

MIDDLE-AGED POLICEMAN: In other words, even though you, the injured party, have plainly indicated to the parties responsible for the injury your wish that they not intrude into your apartment . . .

MAN: Naturally I've indicated it.

MIDDLE-AGED POLICEMAN: The offenders have brutally ignored or resisted the wishes of the injured party . . .

MAN: Ignored is a mild word for it.

MIDDLE-AGED POLICEMAN: Have you got any proof?

MAN: Proof?

YOUNG POLICEMAN: Have you any evidence of violence a doctor might be able to put in a medical certificate—broken bones or bruises?

MAN (*losing his temper*) : I don't need any such evidence. All you have to do is look. They're eight against one.

MIDDLE-AGED POLICEMAN (*considers this seriously*) : Eight against one and not a single bone broken? That makes it a little harder to prove violence, doesn't it?

MAN does not speak and the YOUNG POLICEMAN *lets his glance run over the smiling faces of the members of the family.*

YOUNG POLICEMAN (*to* MIDDLE-AGED POLICEMAN) : The question would seem to arise, rather, why the complainant should have conceived such hostility towards these people —his motives, I mean.

MAN (*dumfounded*) : Do you suspect *me?*

MIDDLE-AGED POLICEMAN : It's not that we *suspect* you. But complaints lodged over private, family matters often create a lot of trouble for us.

MAN (*in earnest*) : This is preposterous. These people are complete strangers!

The members of the family, exchanging glances, smile sadly; one or two rub their chins as much as to say, "There he goes again!" and others wink at the policemen, enlisting their support. All remain silent as before.

MIDDLE-AGED POLICEMAN (*to* YOUNG POLICEMAN) : What are we to do about this, anyway?

YOUNG POLICEMAN (*to* MAN) : I'd be glad to offer my services in helping to patch up the difficulties amicably.

MAN (*almost writhing with impatience*) : Why can't you trust what I say? I tell you I have absolutely no connection with these people. It doesn't make sense to talk of patching up our difficulties amicably.

YOUNG POLICEMAN : That's a little hard to believe.

MIDDLE-AGED POLICEMAN : Have you any positive evidence that these people are strangers, as you claim?

MAN: Why don't you ask them?

The members of the family maintain their smiles intact. They even contrive to mingle a subtle suggestion of embarrassment in their smiles, exactly as if they were sympathizing with the policemen's predicament, or feeling embarrassment themselves over the deranged behavior of one of their own family.

MIDDLE-AGED POLICEMAN: That won't be necessary. I think I've got a pretty good idea of the essential points. It's my conclusion that there has been no injury to speak of.

MAN (*so enraged he stammers*): I'm disgusted. What more can I say to convince you? . . . And if you go on insisting that there has been no injury, even after what's happened, well, there's nothing left for me to say.

MIDDLE-AGED POLICEMAN: Excuse me for mentioning it, but you wouldn't be suffering from a persecution complex, would you?

MAN (*to* SUPERINTENDENT): You can tell them, ma'am, can't you? You know I'm the one who's always paid the rent. And the name—the apartment is registered in my name, and letters are delivered regularly here to me, under my name. That's right, isn't it? This is my apartment. There's no doubt about it. I'm the only one with any rights here. That's correct, isn't it? You can surely vouch for me, can't you?

SUPERINTENDENT (*irritated*): Well, I can't say for sure.

MAN: You can't say for sure?

SUPERINTENDENT: I've always made it my practice, as long as a tenant pays the rent promptly each month, never to butt into his private life.

MAN: But at least I can ask you to vouch for the fact that I am the tenant.

SUPERINTENDENT: I'd rather not go into such things, but you

know, in a place like this the person living in an apartment
isn't always the same as the person who pays the rent.

MIDDLE-AGED POLICEMAN: I can imagine.

SUPERINTENDENT: Take the case of a young, unmarried woman,
living alone . . .

At once FATHER *and* YOUNGER SON *react, but they restrain
each other and instantly revert to the virtuous smiles they
have displayed up to now.* GRANDMOTHER *begins to search
the desk drawer.*

MIDDLE-AGED POLICEMAN: Hmmm. I see.

SUPERINTENDENT: In extreme cases we may be sent money
orders without even the sender's name.

MAN (*furious*): But I . . . I signed and sealed the contract,
didn't I?

MIDDLE-AGED POLICEMAN: Come, now. You mustn't get so excited. Of course I understand your problem, but if there's
no injury worth reporting at this stage . . .

MAN: But it's illegal entry, isn't it? It's trespassing, isn't it?

YOUNG POLICEMAN: We always ask the concerned parties in
such private disputes to try to settle them among themselves. The police have their hands full as it is, what with
the shortage of men.

MAN: I've told you, haven't I, these people are total strangers.

MIDDLE-AGED POLICEMAN: Well, in the event you suffer any
specific injuries, please don't hesitate to get in touch with
us again. (*He winks to the family, as much as to say that
he has sized up the situation perfectly.*) It doesn't look as
if I can write a charge—it won't make a case. I'm sorry
to have bothered you all.

MOTHER (*as if the thought has suddenly struck her*): Oh, are
you leaving so soon? And to think I haven't even offered
you so much as a cup of tea.

MIDDLE-AGED POLICEMAN: Please don't bother.

MAN (*utterly bewildered*): But . . . just a second . . . what do

you mean by . . . I've never heard of such a damned stupid
. . . What am I going to . . . it's crazy. No matter how you
look at it.

The SUPERINTENDENT *and the policemen ignore* MAN, *who
runs after them as if to implore their help. They go out
very quickly and shut the door behind them. Once outside
they exchange sarcastic grimaces and exit at once.*

. . . SCENE SIX

YOUNGER SON *strikes a chord on his guitar, as if by way of a
signal. The smiles that seemed to have been imprinted on the
eight faces of the family are instantly replaced by their normal
expressions.*

FATHER (*consolingly*): That, my friend, is what people mean
   when they talk of good, common sense.
ELDER SON: Good, common sense, and at the same time, ac-
   complished fact.
GRANDMOTHER: The proof of the pudding is in the eating.
ELDEST DAUGHTER: It seems to come as quite a shock to him.
   He's still standing there in a daze.
MOTHER: It'll do him good to have such an experience once.
YOUNGEST DAUGHTER: I don't understand him. Why, even a
   child knows how lonely it is to be without friends.
YOUNGER SON: His whole outlook's warped. He's bluffing, that's
   all.
MIDDLE DAUGHTER: I wish it wouldn't take him so long to
   understand what a miserable thing loneliness is, and how
   lucky he is to have us . . . (*She seems to be addressing
   herself to* MAN *only. She wraps the long peel from the
   carrot around her neck.*)

MAN (*suddenly turning on her*): I've had all I can stand of your meddling.

FATHER (*as if reasoning with himself*): It's certainly irritating, but this is no time to lose my temper. Patient care is the only way to treat the sick.

MIDDLE DAUGHTER: Would you like a glass of water?

MAN (*unmoved*): Stop bothering me! I swear, I'll get rid of you, if it's the last thing I do. You can make up your minds to that! I tell you I won't stand being humiliated this way!

MIDDLE DAUGHTER (*unwrapping the carrot peel around her neck*): If we don't do something about it, the broken necklace will never be the same again. Isn't there anything we can do to convince him of our sincerity?

ELDEST DAUGHTER: Humpf. Such exquisite sensitivity!

MIDDLE DAUGHTER (*with an abrupt shift of mood*): Don't act so sour!

FATHER: Now, now—don't forget, anybody who creates dissension or starts a quarrel must pay a fine.

GRANDMOTHER (*still rummaging through the desk, but her tone is magnanimous*): It's a long lane that has no turning . . . There's nothing worth making a fuss over.

MIDDLE DAUGHTER (*to* YOUNGEST DAUGHTER): Come on, help me in the kitchen.

GRANDMOTHER (*sharply*): This time don't do any nibbling on the sly. It's disgraceful.

YOUNGEST DAUGHTER *sticks out her tongue, then exits with* MIDDLE DAUGHTER.

MAN (*suddenly becoming aware of Grandmother's suspicious activities*): It's all very well for you to talk, but what are you doing there, anyway?

GRANDMOTHER: I was just looking for a cigarette.

MAN: Cut it out! Stop acting like a sneak thief!

GRANDMOTHER (*with exaggerated dismay*): Oh—I'm a sneak thief, am I?

FATHER: Of course you're not a sneak thief. I ask you all to refrain from making remarks that might cast aspersions on anyone else's character.

ELDER SON: How about setting a fine of 100 yen on any remark which is decided by majority vote to be offensive?

FATHER: An excellent suggestion. Yes, that appeals to me. There's no such thing as being too discreet when it concerns a person's character, is there?

GRANDMOTHER (*more engrossed than ever in her search for cigarettes*): Imagine calling me a sneak thief! A cigarette only turns to smoke, no matter who smokes it.

MAN: Stop rummaging that way through my desk!

> MAN, *thinking he will stop* GRANDMOTHER, *steps forward automatically, only for* ELDER SON *to stick out his foot adroitly and trip him.* MAN *flops down magnificently.*

ELDER SON: Oops—excuse me!

> *The family at once rushes over to* MAN *in a body and surrounds him, lifting him to his feet, massaging his back, brushing the dust from his suit, and otherwise showering him with extreme attentions.*

ELDEST DAUGHTER: Are you sure you're all right?

MOTHER: You haven't hurt yourself?

YOUNGER SON: Can you stand okay?

GRANDMOTHER: No pain anywhere?

FATHER: No broken bones?

MAN (*freeing himself*): Lay off, for God's sake!

ELDER SON (*apologetically*): I'm sorry. I was just worried you might get so carried away by your feelings you would resort to violence.

MAN: Wouldn't you describe what you did as violence?

ELDER SON: Not in the least. It was a precaution against violence.

YOUNGER SON (*cheerfully*): We won't let you get away with

that! Allowing yourself to get involved in a quarrel is just the same as starting one. You'll have to pay a fine. Or would you rather make amends in kind?

ELDER SON (*dejectedly*): I don't have to tell you how hard up I am for money.

ELDEST DAUGHTER: But even if he prefers to make amends in kind, it won't be easy. How can anybody trip himself?

YOUNGER SON: Can't you think of anything better to do than butt into other people's business? Do you plan to go on removing nail polish forever? It's just a matter of time before you dissolve your fingertips. (*To* MAN.) I wonder if you'd mind tripping my brother back?

MAN (*angrily*): Don't be an idiot!

YOUNGER SON: It can't be helped, then. I'll take over as your substitute.

As soon as YOUNGER SON *finishes speaking he gets up and deftly trips* ELDER SON, *who tumbles over with a loud groan.* YOUNGER SON *at once drags* ELDER SON *to his feet, only to trip him again, without allowing him an instant's respite. He repeats this a third time, and is about to trip him a fourth time when* MAN, *unable to endure any more, cries out.*

MAN: That's enough, for God's sake!

MOTHER (*relieved*): At last, he's forgiven you.

ELDER SON (*grimacing with pain and rubbing the small of his back*): Thanks.

YOUNGER SON: Well, what do you know? Perspiring seems to have relieved my hangover a little.

GRANDMOTHER (*suddenly*): I've found them! (*She clutches a package of cigarettes.*)

MAN *takes a step in her direction only to remember immediately what happened to him the last time. He stops in his tracks.* FATHER *can't quite allow* GRANDMOTHER *to get away with it and takes away the cigarettes.*

FATHER: That's going too far, Mother.

MAN: Sneaking around my desk like a cat. She's a regular cat
burglar! (*He puts out his hand, expecting to get back his
cigarettes as a matter of course.*)

FATHER (*withdrawing his hand, sounding surprised*): What
did you just say?

MAN *does not speak.*

GRANDMOTHER: He called me a cat burglar!

FATHER: A cat burglar!

ELDER SON (*calmly*): That calls for a fine. Number one, right?

FATHER (*his voice is strained*): I see . . . Without warning.
it's come to this . . . I may seem a little too much of a
stickler for the rules, but if we hope to live together
amicably . . .

ELDER SON: Yes, a rule's a rule . . .

ELDEST DAUGHTER (*massaging her face*): Just a minute. There's
nothing to get so upset about.

GRANDMOTHER (*getting angry*): You're always trying to be
different from everyone else.

ELDEST DAUGHTER (*ignoring her*): I think cats are sweet. I
adore them. They're the most aristocratic of all animals.

ELDER SON: But there's a big difference between cats and cat
burglars, isn't there?

ELDEST DAUGHTER: And there's also a big difference between ·
burglars and cat burglars.

GRANDMOTHER (*excited*): Then you say I'm a cat?

ELDEST DAUGHTER: Don't be so conceited, Grandmother!

GRANDMOTHER: But that's what he said . . . He plainly called
me a cat burglar.

ELDEST DAUGHTER: I'm sure he meant it as a compliment.

FATHER: Now wait, please. The meaning is quite different;
depending on whether the emphasis was on burglar or on
cat. In other words, did he mean a cat that resembled a
burglar, or a burglar that resembled a cat?

GRANDMOTHER: I don't care what he said, I'm not a cat.

YOUNGER SON: That's so, I guess. If you were a cat, Grandma, that'd make us all half-breed cats.

FATHER: Therefore the logical meaning must be a cat-like burglar.

ELDER SON: That rates a fine, doesn't it?

ELDEST DAUGHTER (*persisting*): Why should it? He didn't say she was a burglar plain and simple, but a cat-like burglar.

ELDER SON: But a burglar's a burglar. The only difference is whether or not the word has an adjective before it.

GRANDMOTHER (*moaning*): I'm not a burglar!

ELDEST DAUGHTER: Do you mean to say that applying a different adjective doesn't change the meaning of a word? Well, that's the first I've ever heard of *that* argument! If a big fish and a little fish, a sunny day and a cloudy day, a decrepit old man and a snotty-faced kid, a brand-new car and an old buggy, a smiling face and a crying face all amount to the same thing, then there's no distinction either between a burglar man and a burglarized man. I've never heard such a funny story.

YOUNGER SON: It looks as if you've lost the first round, brother. Eh?

ELDER SON: A woman's superficial cleverness, that's all it is.

ELDEST DAUGHTER (*assertively*): A cat is a superb animal.

MOTHER (*indifferently*): I don't like cats.

ELDEST DAUGHTER (*her tone is extremely objective*): They say that a dislike of cats is the mark of an egoist.

YOUNGEST DAUGHTER (*sticking her head in from the kitchen*): But people who don't like cats often act like them.

YOUNGER SON: You don't say! That's not bad, you know.

MOTHER (*to* YOUNGEST DAUGHTER): Little children should be seen, not heard.

YOUNGEST DAUGHTER: Hurry up and help us in the kitchen.

ELDEST DAUGHTER: I have more important things to do. We're having a serious discussion.

GRANDMOTHER: Anyway, I'm not a cat.

ELDEST DAUGHTER (*her tone becoming hysterical*): Stop it, won't you? I can't stand you speaking so sneeringly about cats.

MAN (*finally having had all he can take*): Won't you drop the whole thing, for pity's sake? I can settle this by paying a hundred yen—right? It's too ridiculous. (*He starts to look in his pockets for his wallet.*)

ELDEST DAUGHTER (*coquettishly*): Oh? But that's cheating . . . After I went to all the trouble of taking your side . . .

FATHER (*recovering himself*): That's right. You don't leave us much to say if you're going to talk in such extremes . . . We still haven't reached any conclusion, after all . . . The situation has become unexpectedly complicated.

MAN: What's so complicated? (*He continues to search his pockets.*)

FATHER: I meant merely that our opinions continue to be opposed.

ELDEST DAUGHTER: Yes. You must remember you aren't alone any more. There's someone on your side. Anyway, cats are absolutely marvelous animals.

MOTHER: But I don't like them.

GRANDMOTHER: I told you I wasn't a cat!

FATHER: There you have the problem.

MAN: What difference does it make? The long and short of it is that I have to pay a fine. Right?

FATHER: But the basic principle of communal living is respect for the opinions of each person.

MAN (*his voice dropping sarcastically*): Is that so? I'm delighted to hear it. I'll be sure to remember that. (*He is still unable to find his wallet, and begins to look rather worried. He takes his coat from its hook on the wall and starts to search the pockets.*)

FATHER (*to the others*): What do you say, all of you? Wouldn't this be a good point to try to put some order into the dis-

cussion? Now, if you'll permit me to express my opinion,
the question, it seems to me, is whether the animal known
as the cat—when, for example, it is compared with the
dog . . .

ELDEST DAUGHTER: There's no comparison!

YOUNGER SON: Still, nobody ever talks of a dog burglar.

ELDEST DAUGHTER: That's because dogs are stupid.

ELDER SON: That's a lie.

ELDEST DAUGHTER: What do you know about it?

ELDER SON: There are police dogs, but I've never heard of police cats.

ELDEST DAUGHTER: Of course not. Cats have a higher social
status.

MOTHER: But, it seems to me, cats are lazy.

YOUNGER SON: Wait a second. Hard workers don't necessarily
get very far.

ELDEST DAUGHTER: That's precisely it.

YOUNGER SON: But if you'll permit me to express my own pref-
erences, I like dogs better.

ELDEST DAUGHTER: They certainly suit you. Let sleeping dogs
lie. Go to the dogs. Lead a dog's life . . .

YOUNGER SON: Don't be too sure of yourself with cats, you
caterwauling, cat-calling, caterpillar . . .

ELDEST DAUGHTER: Every dog has his day.

YOUNGER SON: Catnip is to a cat as cash to a whore in a cat-
house.

ELDEST DAUGHTER: Dog eat dog. Die like a dog. Dog in the
manger.

ELDER SON: You see—friends and foes are all confused. A majority decision is the only way, Father.

MAN: I wish you'd drop the whole thing. A majority decision!
(*He is still searching frantically.*)

ELDER SON: At this rate we'll never get to eat dinner.

MIDDLE DAUGHTER: (*emerging from the kitchen with a frying
pan in her hand*): Sorry to keep you waiting. Dinner will

be ready in just a few minutes. Sis, please help me dish out the food.

MAN (*pauses in his search, with vehemence*): Dinner—of all the crazy nonsense! What crass nerve, here, in my house! Listen, I warn you, I intend to use every means at my disposal to obstruct anything you do. (*To* MIDDLE DAUGHTER.) Get rid of that mess. Throw it in the garbage can, now!

MIDDLE DAUGHTER (*recoiling*): But that would be a terrible waste!

FATHER (*looks into the frying pan*): Mmm. It certainly smells good.

ELDER SON: I'm convinced that food is meant to be eaten with lots of company. Nothing is drearier than shoveling in a quick meal. I can tell you that from my own personal experience.

MAN: Unfortunately, there are some people whose temperament is such that they prefer to live alone.

ELDER SON: Well, I can see that once you've argued yourself into a point of view you'd want to stick to it.

While they are talking MIDDLE DAUGHTER *exits.*

ELDEST DAUGHTER: My sister used to take a course in cooking. (*At last she gets up and starts toward the kitchen.*)

GRANDMOTHER (*to* ELDEST DAUGHTER): I'm in charge of dividing up the jam.

ELDEST DAUGHTER: It's quite something to have been able to make a curry with the ingredients she had. (*She exits.*)

YOUNGER SON (*stifling a yawn*): I feel more like sleeping than eating now . . . My hangover is beginning to take its toll.

GRANDMOTHER: I'm no good without my food. I can't get to sleep without first putting my tapeworm to bed.

MAN (*strangely self-possessed*): In that case, you should stay awake all the time. Stay awake for years, or maybe dozens of years, as long as you like. I warned you, didn't I, that I intend to do everything in my power to obstruct you? That wasn't an empty threat. I assure you I intend to carry it out. I'll make sure you don't get to eat even a slice of bread.

GRANDMOTHER: Why won't we?

ELDER SON (*with a faint smile*): He talks exactly as if he's turned into a magician or something, doesn't he?

MAN (*walking toward the kitchen*): You're going to laugh on the wrong side of your faces!

MOTHER (*to the people in the kitchen, in a casual voice*): You've put away everything harmful, haven't you?

MIDDLE DAUGHTER (*from the kitchen*): Of course we have. I've hidden everything—the tile cleanser, the rat poison, the cockroach spray. They're in a safe place.

YOUNGER SON (*in a loud voice*): It might be a good idea, while you're at it, to stow away the detergents and soap powder too.

MIDDLE DAUGHTER: Right.

MAN *stops in his tracks in dumb confusion at the kitchen door.*

ELDER SON: You see! He intended to use one of them.

YOUNGER SON (*to* MAN): You planned to use a spray to squirt foam over the dinner, didn't you?

FATHER (*a consoling expression on his face*): For good or for evil, everybody tends to think, more or less, along the same lines.

YOUNGER SON: Foam—that reminds me—beer! (*As if appealing for sympathy he looks up at ceiling.*)

While the preceding conversation has been going on MOTHER *has at last finished removing her make-up. She puts away her beauty aids and, rising to her feet, turns to face the others. All of a sudden she takes hold of her hair and pulls up, to reveal she is wearing a wig. She blows into the wig, fans it with her hand, and after shaking it out thoroughly, puts it back on her head.*

MOTHER (*to* MAN, *with an artificial laugh*): You don't mind, do you? You're not a stranger any more, after all. (*Abruptly changing her tone.*) By the way, what ever happened to the fine we were talking about?

FATHER (*perplexed*): We didn't seem to be able to reach any conclusion in our discussion of cats, and the person in question doesn't seem very enthusiastic about a majority decision.

MAN (*searching frantically through all his pockets, and even in the cuffs of his trousers, with an intense display of determination*): I'll pay, I tell you. You don't suppose I want to be in your debt for a mere hundred yen! I'm paying, not because I recognize I was at fault, but simply because I don't feel like arguing over anything so extremely stupid.

The attention of the entire family is at last attracted by his distraught actions, and they observe him carefully. MAN *suddenly stops searching, as if he found what he was looking for.*

MAN: Damn it! That's funny . . .

MOTHER: Was it your wallet? Or do you carry your money loose?

MAN: I carried it in a wallet with my monthly ticket . . . I can't imagine . . .

The glances of the others converge at the same moment in accord on ELDER SON. *He returns their gaze. There is a moment of silence.*

ELDER SON: What's the matter with you all? Have I done something wrong?

YOUNGER SON (*crooking his index finger to suggest a robber with a gun*): Did you do it, brother?

ELDER SON (*with feigned innocence*): What are you talking about, anyway?

FATHER (*uneasily*): It's not true, is it? I'm sure you wouldn't

stoop to that sort of thing . . . At a critical moment like
this we must, above all, show the greatest respect for the
integrity of the individual.

YOUNGER SON: But he's got a criminal record, you know.

ELDER SON: Stop it! You're ruining my reputation!

*At this juncture the people in the kitchen begin to stick out
their heads and observe what is going on.*

YOUNGER SON: Everybody of course has committed youthful
indiscretions.

ELDER SON: Haven't I told you I've completely washed my
hands of all that?

MOTHER: Please. Look into Mother's eyes. Yes, look straight
into my eyes.

ELDER SON: I've come back to you, haven't I? You can see that
I have . . . I learned, so well it hurt me, how wonderful it
is when people can trust one another and what a blessing it
is when people who trust one another can live together. So
I came back to you, from that horrible world where every
man is a stranger . . . Do you think I'd betray you all? No,
stop it, please . . . As far as I'm concerned, the one thing
that makes life worth living is being together, hand in hand.

GRANDMOTHER (*apparently unimpressed*): You aren't trying to
make us cry, are you?

ELDER SON: I'm serious. I assure you.

YOUNGER SON: I'll bet if ever I tried to lie seriously I could
really warm up to it.

ELDER SON (*uncertain how he should react to this comment, betraying his confusion momentarily*): I understand the situation perfectly . . . And I'm glad . . . I don't feel in the
least offended. I'm flattered you should retain such a high
opinion of my former skill.

MOTHER (*brooding*): Then, you mean . . .

ELDER SON: I leave it to your imagination.

FATHER (*embarrassed*): That won't do . . . You, better than anyone else, are in the position to put the matter straight. How can you speak of leaving it to our imagination? I thought we had promised not to recognize private prerogatives when it came to money.

ELDEST DAUGHTER: Yes, he himself was the first to propose that.

YOUNGER SON (*as if reading aloud*): As previously agreed, in cases where suspicions have been aroused with respect to monetary matters, no one, whosoever he may be, for whatever reason, may refuse a request for a body search.

GRANDMOTHER: Love flies out the window when poverty comes in at the door.

FATHER: I can't understand it. You have the best brains of the lot of us, there's no getting around it. And you're amenable to reason. We all depend on you. It's really intolerable that we should have to treat you like a defendant in court.

ELDER SON (*laughs*): You have nothing to worry about.

FATHER (*relieved*): Then you're innocent?

MOTHER: You should have set our minds at rest sooner.

ELDER SON: I mean, I haven't done anything that warrants a physical examination.

ELDER SON *suddenly raises his hand and reveals that he is holding Man's wallet. The following dialogue by members of the family occurs almost simultaneously.*

MOTHER: You took it, then!

ELDEST DAUGHTER: You've got to keep your eye on him every minute.

YOUNGEST DAUGHTER: Take me on as your apprentice, won't you?

YOUNGER SON: Now I know why you're never short of cigarette money.

MOTHER (*firmly*): Hand it over, here!

As MOTHER *steps forward,* MAN *springs to his feet with an incomprehensible cry and makes a grab for Elder Son's hand. The wallet instantly disappears.*

MAN (*carried away, searching Elder Son's pockets*): What've you done with it? Give it back!

ELDER SON: Oh, you're tickling me! (*He holds up his hands, as before a gunman, and twists himself free.*)

MOTHER (*severely*): You know the rules, don't you? I take charge of the safe.

ELDER SON (*to* MAN): I surrender! If you would kindly look in the right hand pocket of your pants . . .

MAN *doubtfully puts his hand into his pocket and with an incredulous expression he produces the wallet.*

MAN: This is it, all right.

YOUNGEST DAUGHTER (*clapping her hands*): He's a regular wizard!

MIDDLE DAUGHTER (*reproving*): You mustn't say that! You're not to admire him.

MOTHER (*to* ELDER SON, *angrily*): Haven't you done quite enough? Surely you can't have forgotten all about your own family.

MAN (*turning wallet upside down and shaking it*): Not a thing. There's not a penny in it . . . (*He stands there glaring at* ELDER SON, *grinding his teeth, for the moment unable to find even words of protest.*)

ELDER SON (*apparently enjoying it*): A pro who couldn't do that much wouldn't be worthy of the name.

MOTHER: I won't allow it—sneaking off with other people's money.

GRANDMOTHER: Like a cat burglar?

MOTHER (*to* MAN): How much was in it?

MAN: How should I know?

MOTHER (*to* FATHER): Don't just stand there, without saying anything. Don't you think it'll set a bad example if we shut our eyes to this sort of thing?

FATHER: That's right, a very bad example . . . Still, I don't understand it . . . I thought we'd thrashed the whole thing out, only to find you're still keeping secrets from us. Why do you do it? It's not like you.

MOTHER: I beg you, don't make your mother any unhappier than she already is.

ELDER SON (*blandly*): That's what you say, Mother, but were you really so confident you could fleece this guy out of his money entirely by persuasive tactics?

MOTHER: Fleece him out of his money? I was going to take custody of it!

ELDER SON (*to* MAN): Are you willing to let my mother take custody of your property?

MAN: Take custody of my property? She could ask till she was blue in the face and I'd still refuse!

FATHER: There's no getting around it. Money troubles are the worst cause of disharmony among friends.

MAN (*his anger returning*): Can it! You've got no cause to call me one of your friends . . . And as for taking custody of my property . . . I'm getting nauseous. You give me cold chills.

ELDER SON (*to the others*): Now you have a pretty good idea of the situation. You couldn't call him exceptionally cooperative. And he's just as attached to his money as the next man. He wants to have his cake and eat it. You'll find he's a hard customer to deal with. Supposing I hadn't used my special talents . . . I can't help being rather skeptical about whether that money would've ended up, as we hoped, in Mother's safe.

FATHER: That doesn't mean you have the right to grab it for yourself.

ELDEST DAUGHTER: That's right. Stealing a march on the rest of us is unfair.

MOTHER: I wonder if a person who always tries to get the lion's share for himself hasn't got something twisted inside him? It makes me unhappy.

YOUNGER SON (*whispering into his brother's ear*): I'll go to

your defense, if you like, for a service charge of twenty
per cent.

ELDER SON : Don't underestimate me.

MIDDLE DAUGHTER (*hesitantly*) : What do you intend to do
about dinner?

GRANDMOTHER : I'm in charge of dividing up the jam.

MAN (*suddenly bursting into a rage*) : Are you still yattering
on about such things? To talk about dinner, in the midst of
this crazy farce! Listen to me. I'm the original victim. Nobody else has a claim on my money, and I want it back.
What possible difference does it make whether he takes
sole possession of the money or two of you take it? It's
illegal either way. The fact is, it's mine, and I'm the only
one qualified to investigate what's happened to it. (*Suddenly he has an idea.*) That's right! The situation has as-
sumed a completely new aspect. My friend, you've pulled a
real blunder. You have enabled me to file a formal complaint. A flagrant act of pickpocketing has occurred. This
time there's no doubt about it. Even the members of your
family will testify. Well, are you going to give back my
money? Or will I have to bother the police again?

FATHER : There's something in what he says . . . As things
stand, your old tricks have boiled down to nothing more
than theft, plain and simple.

MOTHER (*sighs*) : You've really done a dreadful thing.

FATHER : You've ruined everything. In order to carry out our
mission of spreading love for our neighbors, we ourselves
must be models of neighborly love.

MIDDLE DAUGHTER *steps forward, seemingly unable to bear
what is happening.*

MIDDLE DAUGHTER (*to* ELDER SON) : Why don't you say something? You must've had some reason, surely? Say something. Don't just grin that way.

YOUNGER SON: There are some things about which all you can do is grin. Wouldn't you agree, brother?

MAN: It looks as if the wolves have finally shed their sheep's clothing. The salesmen for Neighborly Love, Incorporated!

ELDEST DAUGHTER (*fiercely*): I'm sick of it. After all we've gone through, I don't want the bother of moving again. (*To* ELDER BROTHER.) I suppose you think you're the only one with the privilege of doing exactly what you please?

YOUNGEST DAUGHTER (*in a low voice*): There's a cold wind blowing outside.

GRANDMOTHER: I don't understand it. What devil got into him that he should have done such a thing?

ELDER SON (*his expression becomes severe*): Your own shortcomings don't seem to bother you.

FATHER (*soothing him*): Believe me, I understand what you've been going through . . . I understand perfectly . . . I'm sure you need more pocket money . . . You'd like to lead a more cheerful life . . . But you must recognize the eternal law that happiness which is for yourself alone is certainly not true happiness . . .

ELDER SON: I am gradually losing my amiability.

MOTHER: The brazen nerve of the thief!

ELDER SON: But, Mother, haven't I been following the ideal of neighborly love? Anything I have is yours, and anything you have is mine . . . Aren't you overdoing it a bit when you treat me like a pickpocket or a thief?

FATHER: I understand . . . I understand perfectly.

ELDEST DAUGHTER: It doesn't help much, no matter how well you understand him. We're the ones who suffer in the end.

ELDER SON: You wouldn't be jaundiced because you can't do as much yourself?

ELDEST DAUGHTER *flares up;* FATHER *quiets her with a gesture.*

FATHER: Depending on the end, a certain leeway is permitted in the means. But the fundamental thing, of course, is the end. Neighborly love is a splendid ideal, but if it is only an ideal, it's a little too abstract, isn't it? Why don't we think it through together? What is the common end we all share?

ELDER SON: I wonder if any of you know how many times altogether I have been insulted in the course of this argument?

FATHER: "Insulted" is an exaggeration. It distresses me you should take it that way. My only hope was that I might rouse you somehow from your errors.

ELDER SON: Would you like to know? Don't be too surprised— fifty-three times!

YOUNGER SON: Fifty-three times? That's a little too precise!

ELDER SON: I assure you, there's been no padding. I made a careful count.

ELDEST DAUGHTER: Isn't that silly? He has nothing better to do with his time, it would seem.

ELDER SON: There! That makes fifty-four times.

MOTHER: When someone of your age tramples the peace of the family underfoot, it's not surprising that he should be insulted a hundred times, or even a thousand times.

ELDER SON: Fifty-five times.

YOUNGER SON *apparently has a glimmering of what his brother has in mind.*

YOUNGER SON: Ah-hah. I'm beginning to see . . .

ELDER SON: Now it's my turn to ask you a question. What are these ends you keep talking about that seem to justify everything?

MOTHER: The family safe is one of them. (*She holds up an unusually large purse that she takes from her suitcase.*)

ELDER SON: What's this? (*He pretends to peep inside.*) Mother . . . there's quite a bulge in the pocket of that purse.

MOTHER (*surprised, looking inside the purse*): Dear me, why it's . . . (*Bewildered, she takes out a handful of bills and change.*) Oh . . . how shocking! (*She gives a forced laugh.*)

The next instant the faces of everybody present except MAN *change completely in expression. Now they are all smiling.*

YOUNGER SON: I was completely taken in, I must say.

ELDEST DAUGHTER: You certainly more than live up to your reputation.

FATHER: I have to apologize . . .

MIDDLE DAUGHTER: Oh, I'm so glad. (*She looks around the family.*) We're all good people, aren't we?

YOUNGEST DAUGHTER: I wonder if I should start practicing too. (*She flexes her fingers.*)

MOTHER: Really, it's enough to take a person aback. He was always a mischievous child, but I never expected . . . (*She removes her glasses and starts to count the money with an air of efficiency.*)

MAN: Hey! Stop it! That's my money! You can deduct the 100 yen for the fine.

ELDER SON *blocks* MAN, *who starts to make a rush for the money.*

ELDER SON: You're wasting your time. I don't suppose you noted down the numbers of the bills or marked them?

At the same time FATHER, YOUNGER SON, ELDEST DAUGHTER, YOUNGEST DAUGHTER *and even* GRANDMOTHER *form a kind of defensive setup around* MOTHER. *It might be effective for* YOUNGEST DAUGHTER *to brandish a cleaver.*

YOUNGER SON: You see how easy it is for trouble to arise over money.

YOUNGEST DAUGHTER: A clever burglar absolutely refuses to touch anything except cash.

MAN (*to* ELDER SON): Your own words prove that you yourself admit that you've picked my pocket.

ELDER SON (*playing the innocent*): I picked your pocket? (*He turns to family.*) Did I say anything like that?

MAN: You weren't the only one. The whole lot of you, without exception, all admitted it.

ELDEST DAUGHTER: I don't know anything about it.

GRANDMOTHER: Do you think any grandchild of mine would ever do such a wicked thing? I wouldn't let him, even if he tried to.

MAN: You're all in cahoots to cover up for him, aren't you? And just a minute ago you were denouncing him so!

MOTHER (*paying no attention to the arguments around her; to* MAN): Tell me, how much did you have?

MAN: I have no idea.

ELDEST DAUGHTER: Pretty careless of him not to know how much he has in his own wallet.

MIDDLE DAUGHTER: A little carelessness makes a man more attractive.

ELDEST DAUGHTER (*darting a sidelong glance at her*): Doing your best to make a hit with him, aren't you?

FATHER (*looking into Mother's hands*): Well, how much is there, anyway?

MOTHER (*complaining*): Not much. 5,600 yen. That's all.

FATHER (*frowns*): 5,600 yen . . .

ELDER SON: I suppose it's just before his payday.

MOTHER (*sarcastically*): I see. I'm sure that explanation suits your convenience.

ELDER SON: There's something disturbing about your tone.

MAN (*not missing the chance*): You see! You're admitting to one another that you swiped the money from me.

FATHER: Young man, if you're going to jump to such conclusions, you'll make it hard for all of us. People often conduct discussions on a purely hypothetical basis.

MAN: Stop quibbling!

FATHER : Well then, shall I concede a point and admit that the money was yours? But you don't even seem to know the amount of this valuable commodity. Don't you realize that the world is swarming with sinister people who have their eye on other people's wallets? The thought of it makes me shudder.

MAN : Wouldn't you yourselves qualify without any trouble for membership in that gang of sinister people?

FATHER : Don't be absurd! We've acted entirely out of good will. We felt it our duty to protect your money by taking custody of it.

MAN (*excitedly*) : What right have you anyway . . . without even asking me . . .

FATHER (*emphatically*) : It's a duty, a *duty*. I have no intention of insisting on any rights.

MIDDLE DAUGHTER (*heatedly*) : Yes. It's true even of companies—they're all making mergers and amalgamations, aren't they? And the same thing applies to human beings too, I'm sure. Two is better than one, three is better than two. The more people put their strength together, the more . . .

GRANDMOTHER : Little drops of water, little grains of sand, make a mighty ocean.

MOTHER (*still looking suspiciously at* ELDER SON) : But there's only 5,600 yen altogether. That won't last for two days, feeding nine people.

ELDER SON (*angrily*) : You talk just as if it were my fault.

MOTHER : I didn't mean it that way.

ELDER SON : After I tried to be smart, and save you some trouble . . . (*In a self-mocking tone.*) This is what they mean when they talk of a man who's fallen so low in the world his artistic accomplishments learned in happier days are his only support.

FATHER (*trying to save the situation*) : What do you mean? Haven't we all been praising your skill, without uttering so much as a word of complaint?

ELDER SON (*going up to* MOTHER): If that's the case, I wish you'd stop giving me that look.

MOTHER (*turning aside and wiping her glasses*): It's a lot harder than you suppose, trying to make ends meet for a family of nine . . .

ELDER SON (*sits beside* MOTHER): I *do* understand, Ma. But I wanted you, if nobody else, to believe in me. In the course of less than ten minutes I was insulted fifty-five times . . . and that by the people I trusted most in the whole world, my own family . . . It was painful, I tell you.

MOTHER (*hesitantly*): Talking that way won't do any good . . .

ELDER SON (*ignoring her; to* MAN): Payday in your company must come the day after tomorrow or the next day, doesn't it?

MAN *is taken by surprise. He is unable either to affirm or deny this.*

ELDER SON (*standing abruptly; speaking as he goes away from* MOTHER): So you see, Ma, there's no need for you to worry over such a paltry sum of money, is there? If people can't live a little more expansively . . .

MOTHER (*with an expression that suggests she hasn't grasped the situation very well*): I know, but no matter how much money you have, it always seems to sprout wings and fly away. (*Suddenly noticing something.*) Ohh . . . it's gone!

FATHER: What's gone?

MOTHER (*to* ELDER SON): You've done it again, haven't you? (*As she stands a 100 yen coin drops from her lap.*)

ELDER SON *flashing the bills ostentatiously, folds them and puts them in his pocket.*

ELDER SON: Received with thanks the sum of 5,500 yen, representing fines collected from all of you for those fifty-five insults. Look, Ma, the missing 100 yen coin dropped on the floor. That's his share of the fine (*points at* MAN). It's wonderful how exactly the accounts have balanced.

They all stand motionless, too dumfounded to say a word. A fairly long pause.

MOTHER (*her voice is like a moan*): Dreadful, dreadful . . .

ELDER SON (*perfectly self-possessed*): Words, like chickens, come home to roost. (*Turns back to* MAN.) I hope it's been a good lesson for you too. Now you know how severe the penalty is for betraying another person's trust . . . But of course, I owe this extra income all to you. It's too late today, but I'll treat you to a drink, tomorrow if you like. There's nothing to feel squeamish about. I got the money completely legally . . . You see, nobody can say a word against it . . . Yes, it really serves as an object lesson.

MAN (*suddenly shouting*): Get out of here! I'll give you the money, only get out of here, now! If it's not money you want, I'll give you anything else, only go!

YOUNGEST DAUGHTER (*playfully*): Do you really mean it?

GRANDMOTHER (*hurrying to the kitchen*): The jam is for me. You promised from the start.

MAN: Go ahead. Take anything you like. Only go.

They begin to take their pick of the things in the room excitedly. But nobody as yet does anything positive.

YOUNGER SON: He's certainly become a lot more generous, hasn't he?

ELDEST DAUGHTER: Do you mind if I look in the other room?

MAN: Go right ahead. Don't mind me. If you'd like the rats in the ceiling, you can have them too. But all this is on one condition—you leave at once. I'll give you five—no, ten minutes, that's the limit. I won't make allowances for even one minute beyond the deadline.

FATHER (*timidly*): I appreciate your kind intentions, but I wonder if two different questions aren't involved?

MAN: Two different questions?

FATHER: Your offer to turn over all your possessions to us, without holding anything back, is more than we dared hope

for. That is precisely the way that true communal living is
to be brought about . . . But when you tell us that in return
we must leave you, aren't you guilty of something like a
logical contradiction?

MIDDLE DAUGHTER: That's right. Living together is what gives
meaning to the act of sharing.

YOUNGER SON: What's yours is mine, what's mine is yours.

ELDEST DAUGHTER: You smell of liquor!

YOUNGER SON: That's why I've been pleading with you to let
me have a quick pick-me-up.

MAN (*turning on* FATHER): You can't have forgotten it was
you yourself who claimed you respect the wishes of the
individual.

FATHER: Of course I respect them. But you're not the only individual, are you?

MOTHER (*to nobody in particular*): If you ask me, there's nothing here anybody'd want. The place lacks the bare necessi-
ties. It'd take a bit of doing even to make it habitable.

MAN: This is *my* apartment!

ELDER SON (*coldly*): This is the apartment *we've* chosen.

YOUNGER SON (*trying on Man's shoes, which have been left at
the entrance*): Well, what do you know? These shoes fit
me perfectly!

MAN *suddenly kneels on the floor. His voice, completely
altered, sounds pathetic.*

MAN: Please, I beg you. Please don't torture me any more . . .
Of course I understand it's all a joke—it is one, isn't it—
but I'm exhausted. . . . I just don't feel like joking. . . .
Maybe something I've said has offended you, but please, I
beg you, leave me here alone.

MAN, *continuing to kneel, bows his head, like a victim
awaiting his sentence.*

The members of the family, struck speechless, exchange
glances. But their expressions are not merely of surprise—
heartfelt sympathy and pity seem to have shaken them.

FATHER: Stand up please, young man. (*He places his hand on*
Man's elbow and helps him to his feet, then dusts his
knees.) It's embarrassing for us if you're going to act that
way. Our only wish is to promote your happiness in whatever way we can, to serve you somehow . . . That's what
first led us to come here.

ELDER SON: Or, it occurs to me, you may have subjectively in-
terpreted our actions as being in some way opposed to your
wishes—clearly, a misunderstanding . . . In other words,
there may exist a difference of opinion concerning means.

MIDDLE DAUGHTER (*enthusiastically*): But hasn't it become
warm in here, just because we're all together this way? It
feels just like spring, even without having our soup.

ELDEST DAUGHTER: Spring? It feels more like summer. Oh, it's
hot! (*She removes her jacket and exposes her bare throat*
and arms.)

MAN (*weakly*): But I like being alone . . .

MIDDLE DAUGHTER: Why must you say such cruel things?

YOUNGER SON (*sounds at the end of his patience*): It can't be
helped. Everybody's sick until his sickness gets better.

So saying YOUNGER SON *begins to strum his guitar. The*
following dialogue is declaimed to the rhythm of the guitar.

MIDDLE DAUGHTER:

>   The streets are full of people,
>   So full of people, they're ready to burst.

YOUNGER SON:

>   But everywhere you go,
>   There're nothing but strangers.

MIDDLE DAUGHTER:

> I'm still not discouraged,
> I go on searching—
> My friends, where are you now,
> My loved ones, where are you now?

ELDER SON:

> They've gone to the pinball parlor.

FATHER:

> They've gone to a bar.

MOTHER:

> To the beauty parlor or the department store.

GRANDMOTHER:

> They're eating eels and rice.

YOUNGEST DAUGHTER:

> They're riding escalators,
> They're going to an amusement park.

ELDEST DAUGHTER (*meditatively; if necessary can be sung to music*): And I have dreams. I dream of a streetcar on tracks that stretch far, far away. A streetcar packed with people goes running away over the tracks. Under the weight of all those strangers packed inside, it shoots off sparks. And in the sparks thrown off by all those innumerable strangers, I am burnt to a crisp, like a little fish forgotten in the oven.

YOUNGER SON (*in a soft voice*): Like a dried sardine, with only little bones.

MIDDLE DAUGHTER:

> I'm still not discouraged,
> I go on searching.
> My shining sun, where have you gone?
> Come back and melt away my loneliness!

FATHER (*whispering confidentially to* MAN): That's why we've come all the way here. We heard your voice crying for help and we searched till we found you through the long dark tunnel they call other people. We wanted to bring you, if not the sun, at least the light from a glowing lump of coal.

MAN (*driven into a corner*): I never cried for help. I . . . It refreshes me to be alone.

ELDER SON: That's conceit, pure conceit! Why, in prison the thing that hits you hardest is solitary confinement. (*An expression of recollection crosses his face.*)

ELDEST DAUGHTER: I'm *completely* hopeless when I'm alone. Even when I'm left to look after the house, as soon as I'm by myself I feel as if I'll go out of my mind.

GRANDMOTHER: It's all written down in Mother Goose. Let me see, how did it go again? (*To* MOTHER.) You remember, don't you?

MAN: I don't interfere with other people and I don't want to be interfered with myself.

YOUNGER SON *begins to play with feeling "The Broken Necklace."* MIDDLE DAUGHTER *sings to the tune. When they reach the second verse the telephone rings suddenly. For a moment they are all startled into attitudes of* tableaux vivants.

ELDEST DAUGHTER: Shall I answer?

MAN (*confused*): It's all right. I'll go. (*He runs to the telephone and grabs it, but he does not lift the receiver at once.*) Will you do me a favor? At least while I'm talking on the phone, will you please keep quiet?

YOUNGER SON: At least while you're talking on the phone? Have we been making so much noise?

FATHER: Shhh. (*He puts his hand to his lips and silences* YOUNGER SON.) Go right ahead. Don't worry about us. (*He*

looks to the side. At the same time the other members of the family strike poses of ostentatious indifference.)
After another brief hesitation, MAN *resolutely lifts the receiver. But he is still worried about the family and his voice is extremely tentative.*

MAN : Hello, yes, it's me. (*Pause.*) No, nothing special. No, I mean it, it's nothing . . . All right, then, good night . . . The day after tomorrow? It's not necessary, I tell you. There's nothing I need your help on at this stage . . . Well, good night. You're going to bed, aren't you? No, it's not that. We can talk when I see you again tomorrow.

Suddenly YOUNGEST DAUGHTER *emits a protracted strange noise in the process of stifling a great sneeze.* MAN, *alarmed, covers the mouthpiece and glares at* YOUNGEST DAUGHTER.

FATHER : Shh!

MOTHER : Do be quiet!

YOUNGER SON : Stupid, isn't she? (*He picks up his guitar without thinking, and the guitar, bumping against something, resounds.*)

ELDER SON : You're the one that should be more careful.

YOUNGER SON : You're making more noise scolding me . . .

MAN : I beg you, stop it please!

GRANDMOTHER : I don't understand. Why do you have to act so secret? We're not hiding from the police, after all.

ELDER SON : It's from his girl.

ELDEST DAUGHTER (*reacting sharply*) : His girl?

ELDER SON : I've surveyed the whole situation.

ELDEST DAUGHTER : But isn't that strange? It's a complete contradiction. After all his insisting that he prefers to be alone . . .

MAN (*desperately*) : I beg you, keep quiet, please! (*Into the telephone.*) I'm terribly sorry. There was a funny noise in the kitchen . . . What? Of course I'm alone . . . A sneeze? A woman's sneeze? Don't be silly.

ELDER SON: I've never heard anything so disgraceful. Stumbling all over the place.

FATHER (*simultaneously*): Shhh!

MAN (*instantly covering the mouthpiece*): I thought I told you to please shut up.

ELDEST DAUGHTER: It may be your girl friend, or I don't care who, but why must you keep our being here a secret? It's insulting.

MAN (*into the telephone*): Just a second, please. There's that funny noise again in the kitchen. (*He covers the mouthpiece*). Think a minute and you'll see why. How can I possibly explain such a thing so that an outsider could understand? It's crazy . . . It'll only make things more complicated if I make a mess of explaining.

YOUNGER SON: Would you like us to explain for you?

FATHER: A good suggestion. We'll have to make it clear, sooner or later, whether we're to ask her to join us or to break with him.

ELDER SON: Making things clear is my specialty.

ELDEST DAUGHTER: It's easier for a woman to talk to another woman.

MAN (*protecting the telephone from* ELDER SON *and* ELDEST DAUGHTER, *both of whom come forward at the same time*): I give up. I surrender. But won't you please let me deal with her? In return, yes, I agree to let you stay here for tonight only. That's fair enough, isn't it? You can use any and all of my apartment, as you please . . . I promise not to interfere in any way with your meals . . . All I ask is that you keep quiet while I'm making this call.

FATHER (*looking around at the others*): He hasn't made any conditions that present special difficulties, has he?

ELDER SON *and* ELDEST DAUGHTER (*simultaneously moving back*): I suppose not.

MAN (*hastily returning to the telephone*): It wasn't anything. It must have been the wind . . . Hello . . . Hello . . . (*He realizes that the other party has hung up on him and dazedly puts down the telephone.*)

ELDEST DAUGHTER: Did she hang up on you?

MIDDLE DAUGHTER: That wasn't nice of her, was it?

MAN, *unable to say a word, crouches beside the telephone, his head in his hands.*

YOUNGEST DAUGHTER: He must really be in love with her.

MOTHER: Don't butt into grown-ups' affairs.

FATHER (*to* MAN): You know her phone number, don't you?

ELDER SON: I know it.

FATHER: Should we call and apologize?

MAN (*moaning*): I beg you, please leave things as they are.

MIDDLE DAUGHTER: Why don't you get to bed?

MOTHER: That's right. It must be about time.

MAN: I don't want you worrying about me. You don't suppose, in the first place, I could get to sleep with all the noise going on here.

FATHER: Of course we intend to retire to the other room. Come on, everybody, get ready!

Hardly has he spoken than the members of the family throw themselves into furious activity. ELDER SON *and* YOUNGER SON *take a hammock from their suitcase and suspend it.* MOTHER *and* YOUNGEST DAUGHTER *bring blankets in from the next room.* GRANDMOTHER *inflates an air pillow.* ELDEST DAUGHTER *and* MIDDLE DAUGHTER *swiftly remove Man's outer clothes. Then the whole family lifts* MAN *willy-nilly onto the hammock.* MAN *shows some resistance, but in the end proves no match for their organized activity. By the time* MAN *sits up in the hammock the family has already withdrawn to the next room. They peep in and throw* MAN *their radiant smiles.*

FAMILY (*whispering in unison*): Good night!

MIDDLE DAUGHTER *sticks out her hand and switches off the light in Man's room. The stage becomes dark with only a spotlight on* MAN. YOUNGER SON *enters on tiptoe and crosses the room on his way to the kitchen.*

YOUNGER SON (*in a low voice*): Beer!

Slow curtain.

. . . SCENE SEVEN (INTERMISSION)

The music of "The Broken Necklace" is played in the lobby during the intermission. Soon afterward the actress who has appeared as SUPERINTENDENT, *still dressed in the costume for the part, makes her way among the spectators, both in the lobby and in the auditorium, distributing the following leaflet.*

An Appeal ....

Some people, it would seem, have been critical of my attitude toward the tenant in Apartment 12. Unpleasant rumors are being spread that I was bought over by the visitors or (what's worse) that I reached some sort of understanding with one or the other of the two brothers and gave him a passkey to the apartment.

I realize, having had the misfortune to lose my husband only a few years ago, there is nothing I can do about it if people, meaning to be sympathetic, say, "She must've needed money," or "She must've been lonely." But I will take an oath that I am speaking the absolute truth when I say that the first time I ever laid eyes on those people was when I saw them in Apartment 12. But in my busi-

ness you get to be a pretty good judge of character, and
I could see at once that there was nothing particularly
suspicious about those people. The tenants in this building are all my valued guests, and the guests of my guests,
you might say, are also my guests. That's why, as I'm
sure you'll understand, I couldn't very well make uncalled-
for remarks simply because there's been some sort of misunderstanding.

I wish also to take advantage of this occasion to confide a
secret, in all candor. To tell the truth, situations of this
kind are not in the least unusual. When you're in my
business you see this kind of thing happening all the time.
I wonder if all the commotion hasn't simply proved the
gentleman doesn't know much about people? I beg you,
ladies and gentlemen, not to be deceived by any false
rumors or to let your confidence be shaken in our apartment house.

THE SUPERINTENDENT

. . . SCENE EIGHT

*The curtain rises to disclose the benches in a public park some-
where. Sounds of cars and people passing make it clear that the
park is in the city. The sounds, however, are filtered and the
buildings surrounding the park are concealed by trees (or something suggesting trees); the spot is somehow isolated from the
outside world. The woman sitting on a bench who seems to be
waiting for someone is the person with whom* MAN *was talking
on the telephone, his* FIANCÉE. *She glances at her wristwatch,
then looks left and right. Her expression suggests she is im-
mersed in thought.*

YOUNGEST DAUGHTER *enters from stage right, skipping along in a way that suggests she is kicking a stone. She strolls past* FIANCÉE. *When she reaches far stage left she gestures as if looking off to the other side of the trees. She strikes a peculiar pose and exits, still maintaining the pose.*

As she leaves, ELDER SON *enters from stage left. Evidently Youngest Daughter's pose was a signal to him.* ELDER SON *struts up to* FIANCÉE.

ELDER SON (*with a slight bow of the head*): Excuse me. (*He starts to seat himself beside* FIANCÉE, *indifferent to her reactions.*)

FIANCÉE: I'm sorry, but I'm waiting for somebody.

ELDER SON: Oh, I see. (*He decides not to sit, but shows no sign of going away. He continues to stare boldly at the woman.*) I was impressed even by your picture, but you're far more charming in the flesh. Oh, you've changed the way you do your hair, haven't you? A natural effect looks better on you than fancy styling. That only goes to show how good the foundations are.

FIANCÉE: I don't think we've met . . . (*Her expression reveals mingled caution and curiosity.*)

ELDER SON: But I know all about you . . . Of course, you make such an impression that nobody who ever saw you once could forget you the second time. It's only natural, I suppose.

FIANCÉE: I wonder where I've had the pleasure . . . ?

ELDER SON: Last night, in the drawer of your fiancé's desk.

FIANCÉE (*at last catching on*): Then it was you last night . . .

ELDER SON (*nods*): Yes, it was. Against my own inclinations I interrupted you in the midst of your telephone call.

FIANCÉE (*sharply*): Have you come as his stand-in?

ELDER SON: Heaven forbid! I wouldn't do such a thing even if he asked me. To tell the truth, he and I have had a slight difference of opinion concerning what happened last night.

FIANCÉE: And you've come to tell on him?

ELDER SON: How severe you are! I wonder what he could've told you about us? I gather from your tone he hasn't been too friendly. I suppose he's trying to clean up the mess he left behind by shifting the blame onto us for that telephone call.

FIANCÉE: What happened anyway?

ELDER SON: How can I answer unless I know the nature of his explanation?

FIANCÉE (*finally induced to discuss the matter on his terms*): I couldn't make the least sense out of him. He was so vague that I . . .

ELDER SON (*with a suppressed laugh that does not seem malicious*): I can well imagine . . . I wonder if the problem is that he's timid, or clumsy at expressing himself, or can never get to the point, or that he's too earnest or too good-natured or too inflexible, or that he's stubborn or an introvert or self-centered . . .

FIANCÉE (*mustering her courage*): Were there also women present?

ELDER SON: Yes, four—no, five.

FIANCÉE: Five!

ELDER SON: But there were men there, too—three of us, besides him.

FIANCÉE: What were you all doing, so many of you?

ELDER SON: It's a little hard to explain.

FIANCÉE (*rather irritated*): But generally speaking, when people have gathered together for a purpose there's some sort of name for their activity. Would you describe it as a meeting, or a card game, or a drinking party? Is there anything that can't be given a name?

ELDER SON: That's the crux of the problem. (*He takes out a comb and smoothes his hair.*) I'd really be most interested to hear how *he* would answer that question. (*He puts away the comb.*) But I've really been making a great nuisance of myself when you've more important things on your mind. (*He bows and starts to leave.*)

FIANCÉE (*standing before she realizes*): Wait a moment! What is it you came to tell me, anyway? You and he make a good pair—one's just as vague as the other. I don't suppose you could have come for the express purpose of mystifying me.

ELDER SON (*sanctimoniously, his eyes lowered*): Of course not. But when I meet you face to face this way I suddenly lose my courage.

FIANCÉE: Go ahead. You're not bothering me.

ELDER SON (*lighting a cigarette; slowly*): To be perfectly honest, I don't really understand his feelings . . . Correct me if I'm wrong, but I gather he's engaged to you and has been planning to hold the wedding in the near future.

FIANCÉE: Yes, he only recently managed at last to rent that apartment. It's more than he could afford, but we needed it to get married.

ELDER SON: In other words, he and you are already as good as married. Right? Why, then, should he have had to keep things a secret from you, of all people, in such a furtive way? If I may cite a rather vulgar example, you often see in the advice to the lovelorn column how a man is extremely reluctant to introduce the girl he's interested in to his parents or his family . . . In such cases is it not fair to assume in general that the man's sincerity is to be doubted?

FIANCÉE: You mean you and your family are in that relationship with him?

ELDER SON: Of course, I don't know how he would answer you.

FIANCÉE (*reduced to supplication*): For heaven's sake, please tell me! Who are you all and what is your connection with him?

ELDER SON (*avoiding the issue*): Oh, yes. I've just remembered. It was something he let slip in the course of the conversation last night, but I wonder if it doesn't give us a clue to his intentions. He seems to hold extremely prejudiced views against any form of communal living, and even with respect to family life he seems to be feeling something close to dread.

FIANCÉE: I can't believe that.

ELDER SON: He went so far as to say that it actually refreshed him to be all alone in a crowd of total strangers.

FIANCÉE: But he's even made arrangements with the movers to have my furniture taken to his place at the end of the month.

ELDER SON: I'd like to believe that he got carried away by his own words. Or maybe he was just bluffing . . . After all, with such a pretty girl like you . . .

FIANCÉE: You still haven't answered my question.

ELDER SON: Oh—you mean our relationship with him? I wonder if it wouldn't be better, though, for you to get him to verify it with his own mouth. I wouldn't want my words to have the effect of implanting any preconceptions . . . It's not that I'm trying to pretend to be more of a gentleman than I am, but I just wouldn't want to make a sneak attack, or anything like that . . . I realize that it must be hard for you to understand, but basically speaking, we're closer to him than blood relations.

FIANCÉE: You must have known him a long time, then?

ELDER SON (*calmly*): We don't set too much store by the past. The same holds true of a marriage, doesn't it? The real problems are always in the future.

FIANCÉE (*again withdrawing into her shell*): Then was it something like a political meeting?

ELDER SON (*looking at his watch*): I'm sure he has no intention of trying to strengthen his position by lying to you . . . He may in fact be planning to use this opportunity to reveal to you his true feelings. Anyway, I advise you to sound him out. Maybe we'll meet again, depending on how your interview turns out.

FIANCÉE (*looking stage left*): Oh, there he is now.

ELDER SON (*showing no special embarrassment*): I hope and pray that all goes well. But I suppose I'm also half hoping that things don't go well. In that case I'll get to see you again. (*Suddenly, as if he had remembered something urgent.*) Excuse me, but would you mind sitting there again? Just the way you were before . . . Hurry!

FIANCÉE, *overcome by his urgency, sits as requested.*

ELDER SON (*with a conspiratorial smile*): That's right. Now I can see the dimples in your knees . . . Aren't they sweet? I could eat them up, those dimples.

FIANCÉE, *flustered, brings together the hems of her coat. At the same moment* MAN *hurriedly enters from stage left. He catches sight of* ELDER SON, *and stops in his tracks with an expression of amazement.*

. . . SCENE NINE

FIANCÉE, *noticing* MAN, *stands and turns toward him as he speaks. In other words, her actions should not start after Man's dialogue begins.*

MAN (*to* ELDER SON, *sharply*): What are *you* doing here?

ELDER SON *turns to* MAN *as if having become aware of his presence only then. Far from showing any embarrassment, he smiles broadly, as if greeting an old friend.*

ELDER SON: Late, aren't you? This will never do!

MAN *looks from* FIANCÉE *to* ELDER SON *and back, then steps forward aggressively.*

MAN: What's the meaning of this, anyway?

FIANCEÉ (*unable to hide her guilty conscience*): It was a complete coincidence.

ELDER SON: But as far as I'm concerned, an accidental meeting that only a marvelous necessity could have brought about.

MAN (*angrily*): I don't know what mischief you've been up to, but you're to get the hell out of here, right now.

ELDER SON (*still smiling*): Don't be uncouth. Well, I'll be saying good-by. (*He winks secretly at* FIANCÉE.) Go to it now, the both of you. (*He makes a clownish gesture with his hand, then saunters off to stage left.*)

The couple stands for a time in silence, still looking off in the direction ELDER SON *has gone. They slowly turn and exchange glances, only to avert their eyes.* FIANCÉE *sits down on the bench, and* MAN *then also sits. Each occupies an end of the bench.*

MAN (*gloomily*): What was he filling your ear with?

FIANCÉE (*looking at* MAN *reproachfully*): Before we go into that, it seems to me you have a lot of explaining to do.

MAN: Explaining? There's nothing worth explaining. It's just as I told you on the phone this morning. I'm the victim. I'm sorry I worried you with that call last night. But even that was their fault, if you get right down to it.

FIANCÉE: So it would seem. It's pretty hard to keep someone from guessing, even over the phone, when you have eight people in the room with you. But tell me, why was it necessary for you to act so secretly, as if you were playing hide-and-seek with me?

MAN: I thought I'd told you. I couldn't think of any way of

explaining in an intelligible manner who those people were or what they were doing.

FIANCÉE: And you're going to explain now, is that it?

MAN: Unfortunately, I still don't know what happened, even now.

FIANCÉE (*a little defiantly*): But I thought you asked me here in order to explain.

MAN (*bearing up under the confusion*): Yes, that's so . . . But my real purpose was not so much to explain as to get you to understand how difficult it is to make an explanation. Maybe I won't succeed in making you understand . . . How could you understand an outfit like that? I suppose that if it happened that I had been on the receiving end of this story, I wouldn't have been able to believe it either . . . I don't know where to start. The only way to describe what happened is to say it was plain crazy.

FIANCÉE (*losing her temper.*): That certainly doesn't seem to be an explanation of anything.

MAN: But have you ever heard anything like it—a bunch of complete strangers, suddenly march in on me without warning, and install themselves in my apartment, exactly as if it were their natural right?

FIANCÉE (*coldly*): It *is* a little unusual.

MAN: It certainly is. As a matter of fact, even the policemen who came after I called refused to take it seriously. (*His voice becomes more emphatic.*) But I assure you, it happened. This impossible thing has befallen me.

FIANCÉE: That man who was just here also thought it was strange. He couldn't figure out what your motive was in keeping their presence such a secret.

MAN: A secret? It's simply that I couldn't think how to explain, don't you see? So he encouraged you to act suspicious. But you're carrying your foolishness too far. Tell me, what possible advantage could there be in it for me to cover up for that bunch of parasites?

FIANCÉE: For a parasite that man just now certainly acted like a gentleman. Unlike you, he didn't say one harsh thing. Why, he didn't even try to justify himself.

MAN: Yes, that's their technique.

FIANCÉE: I understand, by the way, that five of them are women.

MAN: Five of them? (*He bursts into derisive laughter. His voice takes on a triumphant note.*) Five women? That's a good one. Gradually I'm beginning to catch on to their tactics.

FIANCÉE: Was he lying, then?

MAN: No, it wasn't a lie. The five women included a seventy-year-old grandmother, a housewife of fifty, and a junior-high-school student.

FIANCÉE (*beginning to lose her confidence*): They certainly make an odd group of people.

MAN: No, there's nothing odd about them. Didn't I tell you? They're all one family—five children, the parents and the grandmother, a family of eight. Five women . . . that's good. You couldn't call it a lie, and it was effective as a trick. You must've been imagining I was involved with some sort of secret society.

FIANCÉE: You were the one who first gave me that impression.

MAN (*with an expression of relief*): When you've seen what the facts really are, they don't amount to much, do they?

FIANCÉE: You can't blame me. You exaggerated so much.

MAN (*resuming his subdued tone*): It would've been easier to explain if they had actually been a secret society or a gang. But when they look so absurdly and indisputably like a family, it makes it impossible to complain to anybody.

FIANCÉE (*dubious again*): But are you sure these people have no relationship to you at all?

MAN: Absolutely none.

FIANCÉE: I can't understand it. Are you sure there wasn't

some reason behind it, however slight? It's hard to imagine otherwise that they'd move in on you like that.

MAN: They say that I'm lonely and that they intend to envelop and warm me in their neighborly love.

FIANCÉE: They've ignored me completely, then?

MAN: No, I'm sure that, as long as you were willing, they'd be delighted to have you join them.

FIANCÉE (*with intensity*): This is no laughing matter.

MAN (*holding his head between his hands*): That's why I told you they were monstrous parasites.

FIANCÉE: Why don't you tell them to leave?

MAN: I have, of course.

FIANCÉE: Firmly? And clearly?

MAN: In a voice so loud it hurt my throat. (*Weakly.*) But it still didn't do any good. It made no impression on them. They have the nerve to say that occupying our apartment is not merely their privilege but their duty.

FIANCÉE (*after a pause, uncertainly*): Is that really all? Is that all there is to it?

MAN: As far as I know.

FIANCÉE: You've explained three of the five women, but what about the other two?

MAN: Stop it! If you'd only seen how I struggled with them.

FIANCÉE: It's funny . . . my engagement ring doesn't seem to fit my finger any more . . . I wonder if I should take it off.

MAN (*bewildered*): What do you mean?

FIANCÉE: I want you to be frank with me. If you've been putting on a show in order to get rid of me, you needn't go to all the trouble.

MAN: There you go again, tormenting me with your groundless accusations.

FIANCÉE: But what else can I do, as long as you're unable to take back our apartment from those people?

MAN: Insult added to injury! If I'm to be deserted even by you, I'll lose the will to fight altogether.

FIANCÉE (*suddenly sharp*): Then I can really trust what you
  say?

MAN: Of course! Haven't I been begging you over and over,
  till I'm hoarse in the throat, to do just that?

FIANCÉE: Then how would it be if I visited the apartment tomorrow with a friend?

MAN: A friend?

FIANCÉE: A man who used to be a feature writer for a weekly
  magazine. Exposés were always his strong suit, so I'm
  sure he's one person who'll be able to tell what's going on.

MAN: Are you trying to spite me?

FIANCÉE: Let the chips fall where they may. I'm only after the
  guilty party. If things are the way you've described them,
  I'm sure the family will be the ones to suffer. You understand, don't you? I desperately want to believe you.

MAN: In that case, I have no objections. There's nothing more
  I want than you to believe me.

FIANCÉE: I do want to believe you.

MAN: And I want to be believed.

Suddenly YOUNGEST DAUGHTER *pops up from behind the
bench and starts tiptoeing off to stage right.* MAN, *sensing
somebody is there, turns around, and, with a shout, grabs
her arm.*

MAN: Wait!

YOUNGEST DAUGHTER (*letting out a scream*): Murder!

MAN, *surprised, releases her arm.* YOUNGEST DAUGHTER
sticks out her tongue and runs off.

FIANCÉE: Who was that?

MAN: One of the five women in the case.

The stage darkens.

. . . SCENE TEN

A strangely shaped male head emerges from the darkness. The left and right sides of the face do not seem to match, giving an impression of madness. This is the REPORTER *who has come at Fiancée's request. (By changing the lighting, however, it is possible to make the expression change to one of extreme gentleness.)*

REPORTER (*abruptly, all but shouting*): Marvelous, isn't it? I mean it, it's really marvelous. This is what I've dreamt of for years, the model of what family life should be, solid and generous as the earth itself.

In another corner of the stage the faces of the members of the family are revealed, forming a group. They begin to sing a chorus of "The Broken Necklace" to the accompaniment of Younger Son's guitar. The chorus gives way to a solo by MIDDLE DAUGHTER *and the stage gradually becomes lighter.* FIANCÉE *stands in another part of the stage, looking utterly baffled.* REPORTER *goes up to* MIDDLE DAUGHTER, *applauding.*

REPORTER: I'm impressed. Yes, impressed. That one word "impressed" sums up my feelings. Tell me, young lady, what is your philosophy of life? (*He takes out a notebook and holds his pencil poised.*)

MIDDLE DAUGHTER: My philosophy?

REPORTER: I mean, what you believe in . . .

MIDDLE DAUGHTER: Let me see . . . Maybe it is to forget myself.

REPORTER: Marvelous! Not to believe in your own existence is infinitely more of a strain on rationalism than believing in something that doesn't exist. (*To* FIANCÉE.) Thank you. Thank you for having introduced me to such wonderful people. I'm grateful to you from the bottom of my heart.

REPORTER, *overcome by emotion, spreads open his arms and all but embraces* FIANCÉE. *She steps back in confusion.*

FIANCÉE: But it isn't as if we'd especially asked them to stay here.

REPORTER: Well ask them now. They're not the kind of people to insist on formalities. (*To family.*) That's right, isn't it?

FATHER: Go right ahead.

FIANCÉE: But I don't think it's necessary any more.

ELDER SON *has been combing his hair and winking at* FIANCÉE. *Now, seeing his chance, he steps forward with a theatrical gesture.*

ELDER SON: Young lady, why do you disappoint us by saying such things? Your adorable lips were never meant to pronounce such uncouth words as "necessary" or "unnecessary."

YOUNGER SON (*singing to the accompaniment of his guitar*): Chase him, chase him, but still he trots after you, that pooch is really sweet . . . (*He suddenly gets down on all fours at Fiancée's feet.*) Lady, I'm your pooch!

FIANCÉE *is driven into a corner of the stage, but ends up by bursting into giggles.*

REPORTER (*suddenly cries out*): No! This'll never do! I mustn't go on procrastinating any more. (*To* FATHER.) I've definitely made up my mind. I'm going to join you. I'd like you to include me in your group. Where are the headquarters? Where should I apply for membership?

What are the prerequisites? The entrance fees? The conditions?

The members of the family exchange meaningful glances.

FATHER: It's hard, after having been praised so enthusiastically, to know how to answer.

REPORTER: Please believe me! I'll keep it an absolute secret.

MOTHER: A secret? We haven't any secrets, have we?

GRANDMOTHER: We're honest people, we are.

REPORTER: I don't mean to suggest I suspect you of anything. But surely your family couldn't be the only people carrying out this great movement?

FATHER: Well, of course . . . The world is not such a hopeless place.

REPORTER (*greatly in earnest*): I understand. You're saying that it's presumptuous for anyone like myself to hope to be admitted to your ranks.

ELDER SON: Somehow I think you're overestimating us a little . . .

REPORTER: Such modesty!

FATHER: What we've been doing is just plain, ordinary . . . Let's put it this way. All we're doing is what anybody with the least grain of normal human decency couldn't help but do.

MOTHER: You might say we're knitting a fabric, not out of yarn but out of people.

REPORTER: Such humility! That fabric will spread as it is knitted, from village to village, from town to town, until soon it grows into an enormous jacket covering and warming the country and the entire people. This is magnificent! Such magnificence, and such humility! I will become your disciple. Yes, I will sit at your feet. But at least you can tell me where I can find the headquarters of your knitting club.

FATHER: If you'll forgive me for saying so, you should act more spontaneously, as the voices within you command.

REPORTER: Then it's all right if I go right ahead as I please, without any license or authorization?

FATHER: Why should you hesitate? When what you want to do is right, you should throw yourself into it, with full confidence.

REPORTER: Thank you!

FATHER: As long as you perform your services with sincerity and devotion one of these days you're sure to receive word from headquarters recognizing your work.

REPORTER: Then there is a headquarters?

ELDEST DAUGHTER: I wonder.

FATHER: I'm sure there must be one. It stands to reason . . .

ELDEST DAUGHTER: But we've never once received word from headquarters, have we?

REPORTER (*surprised*): Not even you?

FATHER: Society is demanding. But that's no reason to doubt the existence of a headquarters—it doesn't get you anywhere. If you want to believe in a headquarters, why, there's no harm in that.

REPORTER: I see . . .

ELDEST DAUGHTER: I don't mean to deny it myself. Either way, it doesn't affect my beliefs.

REPORTER: Ah? Your beliefs? (*He gets his notebook ready.*) I wonder if I might trouble you to tell me a little about them.

ELDEST DAUGHTER (*emphasizing the importance of her words*): Ask not, but give . . . That sums them up in a nutshell.

REPORTER: Ask not, but give . . . That's quite something . . . Ask not, but give . . . Isn't that splendid? How can any man be so obstinate, even after you've said *that* to him? It beats me. A feast is set before him and he refuses to eat! What a disgrace! Something must have happened to his head!

Suddenly MAN, *who has been lying in the hammock, sits up.*

MAN : Give? Don't make me laugh! What have they ever given me? The dirty swine!

REPORTER : Who's that?

FATHER : You might call him a kind of blotting paper, I suppose.

REPORTER : Blotting paper?

ELDEST DAUGHTER (*going up to* MAN) : That's right. I've never seen anyone so unresponsive.

REPORTER : Repulsive, isn't he?

The stage becomes dark again, leaving light only on MAN *and* ELDEST DAUGHTER. *She produces a small bottle of whisky from the pocket of her dressing gown and takes a swig.*

ELDEST DAUGHTER : Come on down, Mr. Blotting Paper.

MAN : At your service, Miss Parasite.

ELDEST DAUGHTER : Do you know why I've never married?

MAN : Today I made the most terrible blunder. I absent-mindedly sent the car pool manager some papers that were supposed to be delivered to the chief of the planning department.

ELDEST DAUGHTER : Speaking of your company, that reminds me—you took your time coming home from work today. Did you stop off somewhere?

MAN : Are you kidding? You and your family took away my pay check, envelope and all. There's no chance of my stopping off anywhere.

ELDEST DAUGHTER : Don't try to fool me. I know all about it. You stopped off to see—what was his name?—the lawyer, didn't you?

MAN *does not respond.*

ELDEST DAUGHTER : He telephoned us immediately afterwards. And we all had a good laugh. (*She giggles.*) Why even the lawyer . . . (*She hurriedly changes her tone.*) But you mustn't be offended. We're . . . how shall I say it . . . we're considerate. That's why, even after we had our big laugh, we decided not to tell you.

MAN: Then, there's nothing more to say, is there?

ELDEST DAUGHTER: I suppose not, Of course, we should have said something, if only to induce you to reconsider your attitude, but we refrained.

MAN: You keep saying you haven't told me, but aren't you telling me now?

ELDEST DAUGHTER: I must be drunk!

MAN: You're running around like a broken-down neon sign.

ELDEST DAUGHTER: What a thing to say!

MAN: Damn him! And he calls himself a lawyer!

ELDEST DAUGHTER (*to herself*): I mustn't be over-eager.

MAN: Anyway, it isn't easy talking to you. There's no getting around it, you're one of the family.

ELDEST DAUGHTER (*in a syrupy voice*): Then, you have some feeling for me?

MAN: Heaven forbid!

ELDEST DAUGHTER: If you're still interested in that girl, I'm sorry for you, but you'd better forget her. My brother's talents as a thief aren't restricted to the contents of people's pockets.

MAN: I can't believe in anything any more.

ELDEST DAUGHTER: Doubt is the door to progress . . . Talking about doors, I can't help feeling all the time as if I'm a door that's been left permanently ajar . . . Please, come down from there. Hurry!

MAN: You know, the lawyer was in tears . . .

ELDEST DAUGHTER (*suddenly laughs*): I gather he was wearing a bandage on his head?

MAN: It's a wonder he can still stay in business!

ELDEST DAUGHTER: It's just a matter of getting used to it. Nowadays it's not all that unusual for a man to be visited by friends like us.

MAN: But the bandage clearly shows there's been violence.

ELDEST DAUGHTER: Even love has its whips, hasn't it?

MAN: The lawyer said eleven parasites had descended on him!

ELDEST DAUGHTER: He must be an even better quality of blotting paper than you.

MAN: What the devil's the matter with this hammock?

ELDEST DAUGHTER: Excuse me, but I'm taking off my clothes. I feel unbearably hot. I suppose it must be the whisky . . . (*She is wearing under her dressing gown only net tights and a short negligee.*)

MAN: If such a thing as hot ice existed—there may be, for all I know, in fact I'm sure there is—a snowstorm in midsummer, sunstroke in midwinter . . .

ELDEST DAUGHTER: The bottle will be empty if you don't hurry.

MAN (*writhing*): That's funny. What's happened to this hammock?

ELDEST DAUGHTER (*as if she has made a surprising discovery*): Just feel me . . . I really seem to be hot and cold at the same time. I wonder why.

MAN: But what the hell's wrong with this hammock?

. . . SCENE ELEVEN

Lights are suddenly turned on in the room. ELDEST DAUGHTER *wheels around in astonishment.* MIDDLE DAUGHTER *stands in pajamas by the wall, near the door of the adjoining room. Her hand is still on the wall switch.*

ELDEST DAUGHTER (*angrily*) : So you were listening!

MIDDLE DAUGHTER (*quietly and calmly*) : Yes, I heard everything.

ELDEST DAUGHTER (*retrieving her gown and putting it back on*) : What a way to talk! Not a scrap of respect for other people's feelings . . . I've never known anyone less lovable than you.

MIDDLE DAUGHTER: But it's something important.

ELDEST DAUGHTER: I don't care how important it is. Who ever heard of leaving the lights burning indefinitely? Why even he looks as if the light's too strong for him.

MAN (*seems rather dazed*) : Yes, it'll soon be morning.

MIDDLE DAUGHTER (*ignoring him; to* ELDEST DAUGHTER) : Are you drunk?

ELDEST DAUGHTER (*losing her temper*) : I tell you, I'm going to give you a piece of my mind if you keep tormenting me with such stupid tricks. I don't care how important you think it is, eavesdropping is still eavesdropping. You didn't listen because it was important. You listened and then you found out something that happened to be important. Why don't you at least pretend to be a little embarrassed? (*To* MAN, *still fiddling with the hammock, unable to get out.*) I'm sorry, really I am . . .

MIDDLE DAUGHTER: Hmmm. Isn't what you really have to apologize for something quite different?

ELDEST DAUGHTER (*worsted in the argument, she adjusts the front of her gown*) : I don't know what you're talking about, but there's something weird about you. (*She goes toward the door.*) Anyway, with your permission, I'd like to get a little sleep.

MIDDLE DAUGHTER (*showing her first emotional reaction*) : No, you can't! Stay right where you are! You're an important witness. (*She calls through the door to the next room.*) Father, brother . . . would you come here a minute?

ELDEST DAUGHTER (*agitated*) : What are you up to, anyway?

YOUNGER SON (*calling from off-stage*): Which brother do you want?

MIDDLE DAUGHTER: Both of you! Hurry! It's extremely important.

Noises from the next room—sleepy murmurs, fits of coughing and the like—suggest people getting out of bed reluctantly.

MAN (*becoming uneasy*): There's been some sort of misunderstanding, hasn't there? I'm sure the misunderstanding will get cleared up in the end. There's nothing to get so excited about . . . But what the devil's happened to this hammock?

ELDEST DAUGHTER (*glaring at* MIDDLE DAUGHTER): After all this uproar I'm sure we'll discover that the mountain labored to bring forth a mouse. You're not going to get away with paying a 100 yen fine this time . . . I trust you've got a good stock of pin money.

MIDDLE DAUGHTER (*quietly*): It hurts me to tell you, but this is no mouse. You mean to say you haven't caught on yet?

ELDER SON, FATHER and YOUNGER SON, in that order, appear from the next room. All look groggy, as if they just got out of bed. Each is muttering to himself.

YOUNGER SON: Damn it! I've got another corker of a hangover.

ELDER DAUGHTER starts to make a sneering remark, but MIDDLE DAUGHTER interrupts at once.

MIDDLE DAUGHTER: He was planning an escape!

FATHER (*at once wide awake*): Escape?

They all show reactions of astonishment.

MIDDLE DAUGHTER (*slowly goes up to Man's hammock*): He was just about to try running away.

FATHER (*turning to the sons*): Running away! Things have taken a serious turn.

ELDER SON (*extremely confused*) : I can see that everything has
not been arranged exactly as he might have wished, but
still.

MAN (*apprehensive*) : That's an exaggeration. The fact is, I'm
here now. Right? Run away? Fat chance I'd have, when
I'm wrapped up in this crazy hammock like a tent caterpillar. (*With an unnatural, forced laugh.*) Run away . . .
why I can't even get out to take a leak. I'm suffering, I tell
you!

MIDDLE DAUGHTER *takes the cord at one end of the hammock and jerks it loose. The hammock at once opens out,
and in the recoil* MAN *drops to the floor.* MAN *makes feeble
sounds of laughter, but none of the others so much as smile.*

MIDDLE DAUGHTER (*helping* MAN *to his feet*) : I'm sorry. Did
you hurt yourself?

ELDEST DAUGHTER (*aggressively*) : So, it was your handiwork,
was it?

MIDDLE DAUGHTER : I didn't want to mention it, but you've been
flirting with him for the past three days, haven't you?

ELDEST DAUGHTER : Don't say anything you'll regret! For the
past three days? Go ahead, be as jealous as you like—that's
your privilege—but if you get carried away to any such wild
conclusions, the rest of us will be the ones to suffer.

MIDDLE DAUGHTER (*cool; to* FATHER *and the others*) : I had a
feeling tonight would be the crisis. So, just to be on the
safe side, I tied up the hammock after he went to sleep.

ELDEST DAUGHTER : That's a lie! An out-and-out lie! Ask him
to his face. He'll say which of us is telling the truth. (*To*
MAN, *seeking his assent.*) That's right, isn't it?

MAN (*hesitates before answering*) : It's true she's kindly come
here every evening for the last three days to keep me
company, but . . .

ELDEST DAUGHTER (*unabashed*) : I've no intention of hiding
anything. I've been trying my best to advertise myself,

hoping he'd respond to my overtures. But to hear you talk, I was inducing him to run away! That's going too far, even for a false accusation.

MIDDLE DAUGHTER (*spitefully*): It's quite possible tonight was the first time you resorted to open inducement. But how about hints?

ELDEST DAUGHTER: Mystification doesn't become you.

MIDDLE DAUGHTER (*imitating Eldest Daughter's manner of speech*): "There's nothing to be worried about. This place and time exist just for the two of us . . . If you pretend that nobody else is here, why it's just the same as if nobody were actually here. Think of the others as being insubstantial as the air . . ."

ELDEST DAUGHTER (*bursts into laughter*): How disgusting! Aren't those the usual clichés every woman uses when seducing a man? Didn't you even know that?

FATHER: What was this direct incitement she resorted to tonight?

MIDDLE DAUGHTER (*again imitating* ELDEST DAUGHTER; *with passion*): "You must give up all hope of getting rid of them. You'll just exhaust yourself with useless efforts. Yes, it'd be better to run away than try to chase them out. We'll run far, far away to some distant place where nobody knows us."

ELDEST DAUGHTER: That's enough!

FATHER: Mm. That was pretty direct.

YOUNGER SON: Even with my hangover I can't help being impressed.

ELDER SON: And what was his reaction to her incitement?

MIDDLE DAUGHTER (*severely*): I felt it was certainly a good thing I had tied the hammock so he couldn't get out.

ELDER SON: What a mess!

MAN (*in confused tone*): But don't you think it's unfair to base your judgments on such a one-sided . . .

FATHER (*reassuringly*): It's all right. It's all right. Please don't worry about it any more.

ELDER SON (*to* ELDEST DAUGHTER): But were you serious in trying to tempt him into such a thing?

ELDEST DAUGHTER (*sulkily*): What makes you think I was serious? Don't insult me. It doesn't take much common sense to see that there's absolutely no likelihood of his running away. This is the most disgusting thing I've ever heard of, making such a fuss, so early in the morning.

MIDDLE DAUGHTER: What makes you so sure he can't run away?

ELDEST DAUGHTER: You don't see?

MIDDLE DAUGHTER: I certainly don't.

ELDEST DAUGHTER: He's the acting department head. His fortune's assured—he's a rising star. He knows better than anyone else, I should think, how important his work is to him. He can talk all he wants about how he likes to be alone, or how he longs for freedom, but one thing he can never in the world do is to give up his job.

ELDER SON: That sounds logical, all right.

ELDEST DAUGHTER: Supposing he ran away from here without giving up his job. He'd have to find somewhere else to stay, and it'd be simple enough for us to find out where he went.

ELDER SON: Yes, that'd be no problem.

ELDEST DAUGHTER: And once we found him we surely wouldn't spare ourselves the trouble of moving in with him, would we? We'd go to help him again, as our natural duty, wouldn't we?

FATHER: Of course. We couldn't neglect our duty. That would be out of the question.

ELDEST DAUGHTER (*her self-confidence quite recovered*): And even he must be fully convinced, after living with us for almost two weeks, how strong our sense of duty is. (*To* MAN.) Am I wrong?

MAN: No, I am deeply aware of it.

ELDEST DAUGHTER (*triumphantly*): Well, there you have it, ladies and gentlemen.

They all strike various attitudes which suggest they are ruminating on the above. ELDEST DAUGHTER *throws* MIDDLE DAUGHTER *an unconcealed smile of derision.*

FATHER: In that case, the incident is not as serious as we had imagined.

YOUNGER SON: Then, I hope you'll pardon me if I go back to bed before the rest of you. I may vomit at any minute.

MIDDLE DAUGHTER: I can't help being worried, all the same.

ELDEST DAUGHTER: The more you talk, the more shame you bring on yourself. Pretending to be an innocent little girl is all very well, but it's exhausting for the rest of us to play your game.

MIDDLE DAUGHTER: But when I heard him say, "All right, let's run away!" I was so frightened I shuddered with fear. I wonder if a man can talk in that tone of voice if he doesn't mean it.

ELDEST DAUGHTER: A mere impression, even from someone as bright as you, is not sufficient evidence.

ELDER SON: Yes, if it was nothing more than an impression.

YOUNGER SON: O.K. That settles it. (*He exits, staggering, to the next room.*) It's probably my liver.

FATHER (*cautiously, observing* MAN): Finally, just as a formality, I'd like to ask the subject of our discussion his opinion. Then I'll adjourn the meeting.

MAN (*gradually regaining his self-confidence*): My opinion? After all we've gone through? (*He laughs.*) That's no longer of any importance, is it? How shall I put it? To tell the truth, it's as if some devil got into me tonight . . . Or rather, as if I'd been bewitched by a goddess . . . I felt when I was talking as if I were singing the words of a song . . . (*To* ELDEST DAUGHTER.) I'm not the kind to flatter people, but I really felt as if I were swimming in a pool of whisky . . . When I proposed that we run away I wonder if I wasn't expressing, in spite of myself, the reverse of what I actually felt—my desire to hold fast to you. (*To* FATHER.) People sometimes say precisely the opposite of what they're thinking.

In the course of the above dialogue GRANDMOTHER, MOTHER *and* YOUNGEST DAUGHTER, *in that order, stick their heads in from the next room. They observe what is happening with expressions of intense curiosity.*

FATHER (*reflectively*): I see . . . Well, now we seem to have heard the opinions of everyone. (*He looks from* MIDDLE DAUGHTER *to* ELDEST DAUGHTER.) How about it—will you agree to leave the final judgment to me?

ELDEST DAUGHTER (*in good spirits, now that* MAN *has flattered her*): That's fine with me.

MIDDLE DAUGHTER: I don't suppose I have much choice.

FATHER (*abruptly gives order to* ELDER SON): Prepare the cage!

They all look astonished. But ELDER SON *instantly moves into action. The other members of the family follow him, displaying remarkable teamwork: some arrange the coat rack in the hall, another produces a lock, another overpowers* MAN, *still another throws a blanket over him. Finally,* MAN, *wrapped in the blanket, is shut up inside the coat rack, which has been converted into a cage. A large lock is hung on the outside.*

MAN *at length manages to stick his head out from inside the blanket.*

MAN: What're you doing? Didn't I promise you I wouldn't run away? This is inhuman! There's no excuse for it. It's inhuman!

ELDEST DAUGHTER (*with an expression of inability to understand it herself*): Yes, really, what's happened? After he assured us so positively he had no intention of running away . . .

MAN: That's right. You tell them . . . There must be some mistake!

FATHER: The thing is, you insisted a little too emphatically that you wouldn't run away.

MAN: It's natural for a man to be emphatic when he's speaking from the heart.

FATHER: You yourself were just expressing the view that sometimes people say the opposite of what they feel.

MAN: That's a false accusation!

GRANDMOTHER: The blind man envies the one-eyed man.

FATHER: In a matter of this gravity there's no such thing as taking too many precautions.

> YOUNGEST DAUGHTER *looks into the cage as if she were watching a monkey at the zoo.* MAN *spits at* YOUNGEST DAUGHTER.

MAN: Get the hell away!

YOUNGEST DAUGHTER: Isn't he awful? Even a chimpanzee wouldn't be so rude.

MOTHER: Don't get too close to him. He's still overexcited.

MAN: Damn it! All your clever talk about neighborly love and the rest was a lot of bunk . . . Not even a slave would endure such treatment.

MIDDLE DAUGHTER (*severely*): There's been a misunderstanding. A terrible misunderstanding. You've taken everything in the wrong spirit.

MAN: Shut up! I don't even want to see your face!

FATHER: Yes, the misunderstanding was definitely on your side. And you still don't seem to understand that these measures have been taken because we earnestly desire your safety and security.

MAN: Understand! You don't suppose there's any chance I would understand that!

MIDDLE DAUGHTER: But running away means disappearing. And that's a much more frightening thing than you seem to suppose. You don't think we could expose you to such a danger, knowing how frightening it is to disappear.

ELDEST DAUGHTER (*still not satisfied*): I think you're over-rating him.

ELDER SON: It seems to be our fate always to have our efforts rewarded by enmity.

MOTHER: In short, the world's fallen on evil days.

MAN (*gasping*): But if I can't go to the office, you'll be the ones to suffer. I wonder if you've thought about that.

FATHER: We don't intend to keep you in there forever. Just as soon as your frame of mind improves, of course we'll let you out.

MAN: Isn't that nice? You expect my frame of mind to improve? You amaze me. Don't you think it's a lot more likely to boomerang on you? Don't you realize I'll get to hate this place more and more?

FATHER: Please, just leave things to me. While you're meditating over your solitude in there, the pleasures of your ordinary everyday life, how you used to go to the office each morning, will come back and the happy memories will gush forth inside you like a fountain.

MOTHER: That's right. Happy memories are generally of quite ordinary things. They leave the deepest impression.

FATHER: And then your desire to escape will drop from you like the scab from a wound that has healed.

MIDDLE DAUGHTER: And your peace of mind will come back again.

FATHER: Now for the blankets.

The instant after FATHER *speaks several blankets are draped over the cage. The stage darkens at once.*

. . . SCENE TWELVE

The stage blacks out completely for a moment, but almost immediately afterwards the inside of the cage is illuminated. MAN *sits, his knees cradled in his arms, and his face pressed against his knees.*

He suddenly raises his head and looks uneasily around him. He listens attentively. Then he lies down on his side in a fetal posture. The next moment he gets on all fours like a dog. He starts to imitate a dog's howling, at which the howling of a real dog is heard from a loudspeaker. MAN *again lies on his side in a fetal posture.*

. . . SCENE THIRTEEN

Now light and dark are reversed: inside the cage is dark and outside is light. It is daytime. MIDDLE DAUGHTER *enters from the kitchen carrying a breakfast tray.*

MIDDLE DAUGHTER (*standing before cage*): Are you awake? I've brought your breakfast.
MAN (*dispiritedly*): Thanks.

> *She puts the tray on the floor for the moment, removes the blanket covering the cage, then slips the tray into the cage from the end.*

MIDDLE DAUGHTER: How do you feel?

MAN: How do you expect? (*He stares at the food, then begins to eat little by little, but without enjoyment.*)

MIDDLE DAUGHTER: You don't seem to have much of an appetite . . . If you don't go out and get some exercise soon—

MAN: What's the weather like today?

MIDDLE DAUGHTER: It seems to be clearing gradually.

MAN: The place is strangely silent. Is nobody here?

MIDDLE DAUGHTER (*sitting down and staring at* MAN *through the bars of the cage*): Father has gone to the miniature golf links. My older sister's at the beauty parlor and the younger one at school. The rest are out shopping, I suppose.

MAN (*entreatingly*): Couldn't you let me have a look at the newspaper, even if it's only the headlines?

MIDDLE DAUGHTER: Nothing doing. We must keep you quiet while you're convalescing.

MAN: You're certainly a hard girl to figure out. Sometimes I think you're kind, only for you to act just as much of a stickler for the rules as the others. Sometimes you seem affectionate, but then you're just as stubborn as the others.

MIDDLE DAUGHTER (*smiling*): That's because you only think about yourself.

MAN (*laughing faintly*): I know, that's what you say. But surely not even you pretend that shutting me up this way is for my own good.

MIDDLE DAUGHTER: But it's the truth.

MAN: I don't believe it.

MIDDLE DAUGHTER: It's strange, isn't it? My head is so full of you that I've never even given a thought to anything else.

MAN (*taken aback*): If that's the case, how can you fail so completely to understand my feelings? I have you and your family to thank for the opportunity to study to my heart's content the blessings of neighborly love.

MIDDLE DAUGHTER (*suddenly dejected*): I do understand. I understand much better than you suppose.

MAN: What do you understand?

MIDDLE DAUGHTER (*speaking hesitantly*): Well, for example . . .

MAN: For example?

MIDDLE DAUGHTER: The fact that your sickness has not in the least improved.

MAN (*his interest aroused*): I see . . . You may be right.

MIDDLE DAUGHTER: If I listen very carefully I can hear it, the sound of your heart flying far, far away.

MAN: Just like a bird.

MIDDLE DAUGHTER: And the commuter's train, your time card, the desk with your name plate on it, the street corner with your company's building—they're all gradually melting away like sculpture carved of ice.

MAN: You do understand.

MIDDLE DAUGHTER (*changing her tone*): Oh, that's right. I was forgetting something important. Here. (*She takes a little packet wrapped in paper from her pocket.*) My brother asked me to give this to you.

MAN (*unwrapping the packet*): From your brother, is it? I see.

MIDDLE DAUGHTER: That's an engagement ring, isn't it?

MAN: It's a kind of metal object. It used to be an engagement ring once.

MIDDLE DAUGHTER (*staring at* MAN *with great earnestness*): Oh, I'm so worried.

MAN: About what?

MIDDLE DAUGHTER: You seem already to have gone farther away than I had thought.

MAN (*laughing cynically*): How sentimental we've become!

MIDDLE DAUGHTER: Sentimental? That's not it at all. I meant to say you're a traitor!

MAN: A traitor!

MIDDLE DAUGHTER: How about a glass of milk?

MAN: Yes, I'd like one. The food today was a little too salty.

MIDDLE DAUGHTER *hurries into the kitchen and returns immediately with a glass of milk. She watches affectionately as* MAN, *with a word of thanks, drains the glass with one gulp.*

MIDDLE DAUGHTER (*holding out her fist; she has something in it*) : If I give you the key to this lock, will you promise not to scold me even if I tell you I love you? (*She opens her hand. The key glitters in her palm.*)

MAN (*at a loss for words before this too-sudden realization of his wishes.*) : That's the easiest thing in the world. Why, if you hadn't been a member of your family, I'm sure I would have spoken first, and told you I was in love with you . . . I'm not saying this just to please you . . . I'm sure I would have. (*He starts to shake.*)

MIDDLE DAUGHTER : Are you cold?

MAN : It must be an excess of joy. And now, for the key . . .

MAN *tries to take the key, but his shaking has become so violent that he cannot manage to grasp it. Suddenly Man's face is shot with fear.*

MIDDLE DAUGHTER : If only you hadn't turned against us, we would have been no more than company for you . . .

Man's shaking suddenly stops. He lies motionless. MIDDLE DAUGHTER *tenderly drapes a blanket over the cage and, kneeling beside him, quietly sobs.*

MIDDLE DAUGHTER : There's no need any more to run away . . . Nobody will bother you now . . . It's quiet, isn't it? You look so well . . . Your sickness must be better.

YOUNGER SON *appears without warning from the next room.*

YOUNGER SON (*putting on his shirt*) : Hey, what're you bawling about?

MIDDLE DAUGHTER : Oh, were you there all the time?

YOUNGER SON (*having sized up the situation from Middle Daughter's appearance*) : So, you've done it again.

MIDDLE DAUGHTER : What else could I do?

YOUNGER SON: You're hopeless . . . But there's no use crying over spilled milk . . . Well, we're going to be busy again, what with one thing and another.

MIDDLE DAUGHTER: He was such a nice man. Really sweet. And so sensitive. At the slightest touch his heart would start to pound.

YOUNGER SON (*brushing the dandruff from his head*): We borrowed in advance on his retirement pay. We've got nothing to complain about as far as our balance sheet is concerned.

MIDDLE DAUGHTER: Show a little more tact in what you say. What I lost and what you lost are not the same things.

YOUNGER SON (*looking around the room; to no one in particular*): It's funny with belongings. I don't know why it is, but every time we move we seem to have more and more of them.

MIDDLE DAUGHTER (*throwing her arms around the cage and caressing it*): If only you hadn't turned against us, we would have been no more than company for you.

The melody of "The Broken Necklace" begins to sound, this time in a melancholy key. The members of the family return in full strength and arrange themselves in a line. They are already dressed for travel. They all take out handkerchiefs and press them to their eyes.

FATHER: The deceased was always a good friend to us. Friend, why were you destined for such a fate? Probably you yourself do not know. Naturally, we do not know either. (*He opens the newspaper.*) Here is the newspaper you were waiting for. Please listen as I read, without the least anxiety. (*He begins to read snatches from the main news items of that day's newspaper, ranging from international events to advertisements.*) Yes, the world is a big place. A big place and a complicated one. (*To* MIDDLE DAUGHTER.) Come, be more cheerful. (*He lifts her to her feet.*) They're all waiting for us. (*To* MAN.) Good-by.

They all wave their handkerchiefs and put them back into their pockets.

FATHER: Nobody's forgotten anything?

They begin to march off. The curtain falls slowly. Halfway off the lighting is extinguished, and all that can be recognized is the laughter of the family.

CURTAIN